—HOW TO USE A—
PENDULUM

About the Author

Richard Webster was born and raised in New Zealand. He has been interested in the psychic world since he was nine years old. As a teenager, he became involved in hypnotism and later became a professional stage hypnotist. After school, he worked in the publishing business and purchased a bookstore. The concept of reincarnation played a significant role in his decision to become a past-life specialist. Richard has also taught psychic development classes, which are based on many of his books.

Richard's first book was published in 1972, fulfilling a childhood dream of becoming an author. Richard is now the author of over a hundred books, and is still writing today. His bestselling books include *Spirit Guides & Angel Guardians* and *Creative Visualization for Beginners*.

Richard has appeared on several radio and TV programs in the United States and abroad. He currently resides in New Zealand with his wife and three children. He regularly travels the world to give lectures, hold workshops, and continue his research.

— HOW TO USE A —
PENDULUM

50 Practical Rituals and Spiritual Activities
for Clarity and Guidance

RICHARD
WEBSTER

Llewellyn Publications
Woodbury, Minnesota

FIRST EDITION
Fourth Printing, 2021

Cover design: Shannon McKuhen
Deluxe Silver Spiral Pendulum and Premium Amethyst Chakra Pendulum used with permission by Lo Scarabeo
Photography by Llewellyn Art Department
Llewellyn Publications is a registered trademark of Llewellyn Worldwide Ltd.

Library of Congress Cataloging-in-Publication Data
Names: Webster, Richard, author.
Title: How to use a pendulum : 50 practical rituals and spiritual
   activities for clarity and guidance / Richard Webster.
Description: First edition. | Woodbury, Minnesota : Llewellyn Publications,
   2020. | Includes bibliographical references.
Identifiers: LCCN 2019055222 (print) | LCCN 2019055223 (ebook) | ISBN
   9780738763187 (paperback) | ISBN 9780738763309 (ebook)
Subjects: LCSH: Pendulum—Miscellanea. | Divination. | Fortune-telling by
   pendulum.
Classification: LCC BF1628 .W395 2020 (print) | LCC BF1628 (ebook) | DDC
   133.3/23—dc23
LC record available at https://lccn.loc.gov/2019055222
LC ebook record available at https://lccn.loc.gov/2019055223

Llewellyn Publications
A Division of Llewellyn Worldwide Ltd.
2143 Wooddale Drive
Woodbury, MN 55125-2989
www.llewellyn.com
Printed in the United States of America

Other Books by Richard Webster

CONTENTS

INTRODUCTION

A pendulum is a small weight attached to a length of thread or chain. It's a remarkable, deceptively simple instrument that can reveal information not able to be obtained in any other way. It can also be used for many other purposes, such as answering questions, continuing spiritual healing, enhancing inner growth, eliminating negativity, sending energy, and setting intentions.

The pendulum is a dowsing instrument. The word *dowsing* means to detect hidden substances, usually with the help of a forked stick, L-shaped metal rod, or pendulum. Many people dowse with their bodies instead of using a dowsing instrument (see appendix).

The pendulum has been used for thousands of years. The ancient Chinese used them to deter evil spirits, and thousands of years ago, ancient Egyptians used them to determine where to plant their crops (Copen 1974, 20–21).

1

In his history of the Roman Empire, Ammianus Marcellinus (c. 325–391 CE) wrote about a plot to assassinate the Roman Emperor Valens. A ring attached to a fine linen thread was suspended over a circular platter that contained the letters of the alphabet. The ring moved and spelled out T-H-E-O. This told the conspirators that the next emperor would be Theodorus. The conspirators were caught and executed before they were able to kill the emperor (*The Roman History of Ammianus Marcellinus*, OOOIX, 29).

Michel-Eugène Chevreul (1786–1889), a director of the Natural History Museum in Paris, spent twenty years studying the pendulum. He concluded that there was a strong relationship between the thoughts of the dowser and the movements of the pendulum. This phenomenon is called the ideomotor response, and shows that suggestion can create involuntary, unintentional, and unconscious movement. The term *ideomotor action* was first used by Dr. William Benjamin Carpenter in 1852. He created the word from *ideo*, meaning idea or thought, and *motor*, meaning muscular action.

In the early twentieth century, Abbé Alexis Mermet (1866–1937), a village priest, became known throughout Europe as the "king of dowsers." He learned the art from his father and grandfather, both well known for their dowsing skills. Using a pendulum, he discovered petroleum in Africa, conducted archaeological researches for the Roman Catholic Church, found water in Colombia, and located missing people and animals in many countries. In 1934, he located the body of a six-year-old boy in an eagle's nest, high in the mountains of Switzerland. This sensational case attracted enormous media attention, and even skeptics were unable to explain how the boy's body had traveled so far. Abbé Mermet's book, *Principles and Practice of Radiesthesia*, was published in 1935 and is still in print today.

The word *radiesthesia* means dowsing, and was coined by another priest, Abbé Alexis-Timothée Bouly. He located water for troops during the First World War, and after the war, dowsed for unexploded shells. He was one of the founders of the Society of Friends of Radiesthesia. In 1950, he received France's highest honor when he was knighted and became a Chevalier de la Legion d'Honneur (Staffen 2019, 11).

The pendulum became popular with the general public in the early twentieth century when it was marketed as a sex detector. In this case, the pendulums were pea-sized hollow metal balls attached to a thread. I have one of these that was made in the 1920s. The instructions, printed on a postage stamp-sized piece of paper, said that if the pendulum was suspended over the palm of a pregnant woman it would move in a circular motion to indicate a girl, and in a straight line to indicate a boy.

During the Second World War, the Germans used dowsers to follow the movements of British warships (Willey 1975, 192). There are also many accounts of soldiers using pendulums and L-shaped rods to locate hidden mines and tunnels during the Vietnam War.

In early 1959, Verne Cameron, a professional dowser, contacted Vice Admiral Maurice E. Curtis and told him he could locate submarines using nothing but a pendulum and a map. He also claimed to be able to identify the nationality each submarine belonged to. The US Navy accepted his offer and watched Verne Cameron and his pendulum dowse a map of the Pacific Ocean. He located all the US submarines in a matter of minutes, and then located all the Russian ones. Despite this success, the navy didn't ask him to repeat the experiment. Several years later, Verne Cameron was invited by the South African government to dowse for precious resources. He applied for a passport but wasn't given one, as the CIA considered him a security risk (many sources, including Eason).

In 1977, a unique experiment called Project Deep Quest began. There were two parts to it. The first part, a classified project for the US Air Force, tested long-range remote viewing from inside a submersible. The second part was unclassified, and involved two map dowsers, Ingo Swann and Hella Hammid, who were asked to locate sea wrecks at the bottom of the ocean in a 1,500-square-mile area near Catalina Island, close to Los Angeles. The two dowsers worked separately, and a composite map was made of their findings. All the shipwrecks that were previously known were eliminated, leaving one target that had been marked by both dowsers. Their sites were only a few hundred yards apart. A previously unknown shipwreck was found in the area that the two dowsers indicated (Jacobsen 2017, 195–200).

In 1991, Dr. Elizabeth Mayer's daughter's harp was stolen in Oakland, California. Despite considerable publicity, the police couldn't find it, and two months later a friend dared the skeptical doctor to contact a dowser. She phoned Harold McCoy, president of the American Society of Dowsers, who lived in Arkansas. She told him what had happened and he checked to see if the harp was still in Oakland. As his pendulum told him it was, he asked Dr. Mayer to send him a map of the city. He dowsed the map with his pendulum and sent her the coordinates of the location where the harp could be found. She told the police she'd received a tipoff, but they told her that wasn't enough to obtain a search warrant. She placed flyers around the neighborhood asking for help in getting it back, no questions asked. The harp was returned in three days. Dr. Mayer was a psychoanalyst and an associate clinical professor with a private practice in Berkeley. This experience changed her life, and she wrote a book called *Extraordinary Knowing: Science, Skepticism and the Inexplicable Powers of the Human Mind*.

PART 1

Some Pendulum Basics

1

◆

HOW TO CHOOSE A PENDULUM

A pendulum is simply a weight attached to a length of string or chain. My mother used her wedding ring attached to a length of thread. A plumb bob from a hardware store works well. A paperclip attached to a length of thread works well when nothing else is available. One of my favorite pendulums is a small piece of greenstone that's attached to a loop of cord. A good friend carved it for me, and it brings back happy memories every time I use it. I wear it as an amulet, which means I have it with me almost all the time. I also regularly use an old key attached to a chain. Commercially made pendulums are readily available at New Age stores and online.

The weight can be made of virtually anything, including wood, crystal, glass, plastic, and some metals. Metals usually act as conductors, which can affect the readings. Copper and aluminum should not be used. Crystal pendulums are especially useful for healing work. Some dowsers like to use pendulums made from the material they're dowsing for.

The best pendulum for you is something that looks attractive and is easy to hold and use. Ideally, it should weigh approximately three ounces. Symmetrical, spherical, and cylindrical shapes work particularly well. Many dowsers like weights that are roundish in shape, but curve down to a point at the bottom.

Some pendulums have a hollow compartment inside them. They are known as sample or witness pendulums. These enable the dowser to put a small sample of whatever he or she is searching for inside the compartment before starting to dowse. If you're divining for water, you can insert a few drops of water into the compartment. Similarly, you'd insert oil if you're searching for oil, and gold when looking for gold.

Almost anything can be used if you need a pendulum but don't have one with you. I've used car keys, jewelry, small novelty items attached to thread, metal nuts, fishing sinkers, cotton reels, and paper clips at different times, and they all worked well. However, you'll find the best results come from a special pendulum that you use only for dowsing or magical work.

At one time I had dozens of pendulums, as my children frequently gave me ornamental items attached to chains or thread as birthday and Christmas presents. Today, I have about ten pendulums, and use two of these regularly. I still occasionally buy myself a pendulum that appeals to me. Before buying it, I hold it by the chain and ask, "Is this pendulum in harmony with me?" If the pendulum gives a positive response, I'll buy it.

Several members of a dowsing society I belong to make their own pendulums. This is a good idea if you have the necessary skills, as your energies will be imparted into the finished pendulum. Choose your materials carefully, and take your time. Even if you can't carve or mold a particular shape, you might find a suitable object that you could attach to a thread or chain.

2

◆

HOW TO OPERATE
A PENDULUM

The easiest way to start using a pendulum is to sit down in front of a table with the chain of the pendulum held between the thumb and first finger of your dominant hand (right hand if you're right-handed, and left hand if you're left-handed). Rest your elbow on the table, and make sure that no other part of your body is in contact with it. Your legs should be uncrossed and your feet should be flat on the floor. The palm of the hand holding the pendulum should be face down, and the pendulum should hang seven to twelve inches in front of you.

If you're experimenting while standing, make sure that your elbow creates a right angle with your forearm parallel to the floor or ground.

Swing the pendulum gently in circles, both clockwise and counterclockwise. After this, swing it from side to side, and toward and away from you. This helps you become familiar with the movements the pendulum can make. Experiment by holding the thread at different lengths to see which feels best for you. Most people find that four to five inches is about right. However, you might prefer to have a shorter or longer length. You should also experiment with holding the pendulum in your other hand.

Once you've become used to the various movements of the pendulum, use your free hand to stop the weight from moving. When it's still, ask it which movement indicates a "yes" or positive response. You can talk to your pendulum silently or out loud. You may find that your pendulum immediately moves to indicate the positive response. However, if you've never used a pendulum before, it might move only slightly, or not at all. Be patient. Keep asking the pendulum to indicate its positive response, and in time it will start moving.

You may find it helpful to drink some water before using your pendulum. In the 1960s, Dr. Jacob V. Harvalik, a physicist and advisor to the US Army, found that dowsing ability improved if the person drank "a few tumblers of water" before starting (Wilson 1988, 116).

It can be frustrating if the pendulum fails to provide an immediate response. If it fails to respond after five minutes, put it away and try again later. Once you've become used to your pendulum, you'll find the responses will come as soon as you think of a question.

If you continue to have problems getting the pendulum to move, forget about asking it to indicate a positive response. Instead, focus on the weight and imagine it moving to and fro. This almost always works. Once you've got the pendulum moving, stop the movement and ask it to indicate the positive response.

Another solution is to ask someone who is proficient with the pendulum to rest a hand on your right shoulder if you're holding the pendulum in your right hand (your left shoulder if you're using your left hand). Again, ask for a positive response, and you'll find that this time the pendulum will move.

I have yet to meet anyone who cannot use a pendulum. You don't need to be specially gifted or have some sort of supernatural power. All you need do is to be patient, suspend any disbelief, and allow it to happen. Keep your sense of humor and ensure that your practice sessions are done with a sense of fun. Grim determination seldom produces good results. Practice for five minutes at a time until the pendulum responds. Once it's responded, you'll never have problems of this sort again.

Now that you've found your yes response, stop the movement of the weight again, and ask it to give you its negative or "no" response. You can follow this by asking it to indicate its responses to "I don't know" and "I don't want to answer."

These four responses will probably stay the same for the rest of your life. However, if you haven't used your pendulum for a while, it pays to check, just in case they have changed.

The next step is to start asking your pendulum questions that you know the answers to. You might ask, "Am I male?" If you are, the pendulum should give a yes response. Naturally, it should give a "no" response if you're female. You can ask similar questions about your name, age, occupation, address, number of children, hobbies, and so on. Instead of asking questions about yourself and your loved ones, you might prefer asking neutral questions, such as "Am I sitting down?"; "Is it raining outside?"; "Is the wallpaper blue?"; or "Is this month July?"

After you've succeeded at this, you can ask questions that you don't know the answers to. You might start by asking questions about a friend who is in the same room as you. This means that you can check the pendulum's responses right away. You might ask, "Do you like broccoli?"; "Are you a good swimmer?"; "Do you speak more than one language?"; or "Have you ever been to France?"

Try this test with different people you come into contact with. You'll find that almost everyone will be intrigued by the pendulum and happy to participate.

Once you've had some success with this, you can ask questions about anything, as long as you're able to find the correct answers later. Here's an example. If you're not at home, you might ask your pendulum what your partner is cooking for dinner. You can confirm what your pendulum told you by phoning or texting your partner, or waiting until you get home.

The internet is a great resource nowadays, and makes it easy to find answers to almost anything. Even so, some of the answers you receive might take time to verify.

Be careful with the questions you ask, as it's possible to override the movements of the pendulum with your will. This is especially the case if you have an emotional involvement in the outcome. Once people hear of your interest in pendulum dowsing, you'll have many requests inquiring about the gender of unborn babies. You may feel you're using the pendulum objectively, but if you secretly hope the unborn child will be a girl, the pendulum will reflect your feelings and tell you that the baby will be a girl, even if that is not the case.

Recently, a friend of mine used his pendulum to see what college his son would go to. He was excited when his pendulum told him that it would be the same college he'd studied at. Not surprisingly, he was disappointed when his son wasn't accepted, and had to accept an offer from a different university.

The remedy for this is to ask someone who has no emotional involvement in the outcome to use the pendulum for you. Another solution is to follow the question with another one: "Was that answer the truth?"

This shows that the pendulum is a sensitive instrument that can be easily influenced by your mind. If you hold your pendulum and mentally ask it to move in a particular direction, you'll find that it will quickly do so. If you then think about a different direction, your pendulum will follow your thoughts and move in the new direction.

Your pendulum should not be used to ask silly or frivolous questions. If you do ask these, you'll receive a trivial answer. If, for instance, you ask, "Am I God's gift to women?" you might receive a serious answer, but it's more likely that you'll receive "I don't know" or "I don't want to answer." You might even find that your pendulum remains still and refuses to move when you ask a frivolous question.

However, don't ask any important questions until you've gained experience with your pendulum. With practice, your pendulum will start moving the instant you formulate a question. Once you've reached this stage, you'll be able to ask more serious questions.

3

◆

HOW TO ASK
QUESTIONS

Before asking any questions, you should symbolically protect yourself. This isn't necessary for most purposes, but it's a good habit to get into. It's essential if you're dowsing for anything that could be harmful, such as geopathic stress. (See use 37 on page 181.) There are many ways to protect yourself. I start by standing with my legs slightly apart and my arms by my sides. I take three slow, deep breaths, then visualize or imagine a pure white light descending from the Universal Life Force (Divine Spirit, God, or whatever name you choose). In my mind, I picture this white light filling my body to overflowing with protective energy. The excess white light forms a bubble of protection that completely surrounds me.

There is an almost unlimited list of questions that your pendulum can answer. You can find out which book or books you should read, choose the right babysitter for your child, find the right house to live in, determine the best place to go on vacation, decide which doctor or dentist would best suit your needs, choose the best time to ask for a pay raise, determine the best day to hold an important event, choose a pet, find out if someone is honest or not, or even find water.

Your questions need to have a purpose. This is known as your intent. If you know precisely what you're asking for, you can frame your questions in a way that will allow your pendulum to answer them.

Don't ask the same question again after you've received a response. Your subconscious mind may try to please you by giving you a different answer, but it probably won't be the correct one.

There's an important question you should always ask before using your pendulum for any purpose. This question is "Is it in the best interests of everyone concerned for me to dowse today for (whatever purpose you have in mind)?"

Many dowsers ask three questions before starting to dowse: Can I, may I, and should I?

"Can I?" asks the Universal Life Force if you have the necessary ability to successfully dowse for whatever it happens to be.

"May I?" confirms that you have the permission of everyone involved in what you're going to do. If you're planning to dowse a house, for instance, a positive answer to this question means that the owner of the house has given you permission to proceed.

"Should I?" ensures that what you're planning to do is in the best interest of everyone concerned. It also ensures that this is a good time to proceed, and that you're in the right state of mind to perform the dowsing. It's not a good idea to dowse if you're hungover, depressed, angry, or feeling unwell.

It can also be helpful to confirm the entire process by asking "Will the answers I receive be correct?"

To help protect yourself, you can also ask if you're sufficiently grounded and if you have enough energy to use your pendulum today. (See use 21 on page 107 if you need to raise your energy levels.)

To achieve the best results, you need to phrase your questions carefully. As the pendulum is limited to four possible answers, you need to ask questions that the pendulum can answer.

Your pendulum can't, for instance, answer a question like "Should I travel to Paris or London?" In this instance, you could ask the question twice, once for Paris and again for London. Alternatively, you might ask, "Would it be better for me to fly to Paris rather than London?" If you wish, you can confirm the result by asking the same question again with the cities reversed.

"Will my business be successful?" is another question that is impossible for your pendulum to answer. Does "successful" mean making the equivalent of an average wage from the business, or does it mean earning hundreds of thousands of dollars a year? This question is too vague. If you're thinking of financial success, a better question would be: "Will my business earn (a specific number of dollars) this year?"

Another common fault occurs when not all of the necessary information is provided. For instance, someone might be using a pendulum to dowse for water. Water will be found at the place the pendulum indicated, but it may not be suitable for drinking purposes. If the person required good quality, pure drinking water, but did not specify that, he or she is likely to be disappointed with the result.

Australian dowser Chris Gozdzik learned this the hard way. When he received a large order from someone in the United Kingdom, he asked his pendulum if the credit card was good. He received a positive response, and sent off the order. A week later, he received two more orders from the same customer, using different credit cards. He contacted the bank that had issued the cards, and learned that they were stolen. His pendulum was correct in saying the cards were good, but he hadn't asked if they were stolen.

It's possible to save time by using phrases such as "instead of," "in preference to," or "rather than." Here's an example: "Should I continue working at ABC Company, rather than accept the job offer from XYZ Company?" If the answer is positive, you'll know what to do. If the answer is negative, you could ask, "Should I accept the job offer from XYZ Company, in preference to continuing to work at ABC Company?"

Most of the time it's better to ask a series of simple questions rather than trying to create one complex question that will answer everything at once. There will be virtually no difference in the time expended, there will be no confusion, and you'll receive a clearer answer.

Occasionally, you'll receive the "I don't want to answer" response. I always take this as an indication that I haven't asked the question clearly enough. I then think of my intention again, and, if possible, ask two or three simpler questions that will lead me to the answer I'm looking for.

Focus on your question while holding the pendulum. With practice, you'll find that you enter a slightly altered state in which your mind is still and you focus solely on your question. You're curious and want to know the answer, but at the same time you're detached from the outcome. If you allow your mind to wander, the pendulum could respond to a passing thought rather than the question you're asking.

4

◆

PENDULUM CHARTS AND EXPERIMENTS

You can create semicircular charts for any purpose. You can divide it into as many sections as you wish, and then suspend your pendulum over the center of the baseline and see what reading it gives for your particular need. If you're planning a vacation, for instance, and can't decide which of four places you'd most like to visit, you could divide the semicircle into four sections and write a name in each section. Ask which destination would be the most enjoyable one for you, and see which section your pendulum indicates.

You can buy books of ready-made charts for a variety of purposes. I prefer to create my own for my specific needs. The chart I use most is divided into ten sections, and I measure percentages with it. Before going to an important meeting, I might ask, "Will I be happy with the result of this meeting?" The pendulum will give me the answer. Hopefully, it will be more than ninety percent. If the number is lower than I expected, I might prepare more material to present, or perhaps decide to cancel the meeting.

Samples

Many dowsers like to have a sample of whatever it is they're dowsing for. If they're dowsing for water, for instance, they might carry a sample of pure water. They'll do the same when dowsing for oil or particular minerals. If they're searching for a missing person, they'll use a photograph of him or her, or an article of the person's clothing. This helps them "tune in" to the person they're searching for.

Some dowsers write the name of whoever or whatever it is they're looking for on a piece of paper and carry it with them, or place it inside their pendulum. (Some pendulums contain a small cavity, known as the witness chamber, where a sample of the item being searched for can be placed.)

Some dowsers always use samples when they dowse. However, most make less use of them as they gain experience. Experiment, and use samples if you find them useful.

Other Experiments

Here are some more experiments that will help you become familiar with your pendulum, and what it can do.

Suspend your pendulum over the positive end of an AA battery and see what movement your pendulum makes. It should indicate your positive (yes) direction. If you move it to the negative end of the battery, it will produce your negative (no) response. If you suspend the pendulum in the center of the battery, it will start swinging to and fro between the two ends. You can continue this exercise by seeing what happens when you hold your pendulum over each end of a bar magnet, and the north and south poles of a compass.

Observe what happens when you cross your hands or feet while you're holding the pendulum. Or place two coins of the same denomination several inches apart and suspend your pendulum halfway between them. You'll find your pendulum will start swinging horizontally to and fro between the two coins. The next step is to place one of the coins a few inches away from a small oblong or square container, such as a matchbook or a deck of cards. Suspend the pendulum between them. This time the pendulum will not swing from one object to the other. Instead, it will swing vertically between the two objects. This shows how the pendulum reacts when placed between two similar and dissimilar objects.

Suspend your pendulum over items made of different metals, and notice the reactions your pendulum has to each one. Try the same experiment with different gemstones, or swatches of color.

You can follow this by collecting an assortment of small objects. You might choose a battery-powered object, something that's connected to your home's electricity, a cell phone, a watch, a crystal, a toy, a potted plant, a favorite book, or an item of food. Hold your pendulum over each of these in turn and observe how it responds. If these are all approximately equal in size, you can ask someone to conceal one of them inside a cardboard box. With practice, the movements of your pendulum will tell you what the object is.

An agreeable friend might let you hold your pendulum over different parts of his or her body to see how it reacts in different places.

Another interesting experiment is to hold your pendulum over the back of your hand or your thigh, and then observe its movements. It will probably indicate your positive response. Take the pendulum away and slap your thigh (or the back of your hand) firmly. Now if you hold the pendulum over your thigh (or back of your hand) again, you'll find that it will give a negative response, indicating the "damage" your slap caused. Check it again ten or fifteen minutes later and you'll find it will have returned to normal and will be giving you a positive response again.

Suspend your pendulum over a glass of water and ask if the water is good for you. You can do the same with any food or drink. Food that is good for one person may not necessarily be good for someone else.

If you have fresh fruit in your kitchen, place them in a flat dish and turn your back. Ask a friend to pick up one piece of fruit and to then replace it. Then turn around and hold your pendulum over each item of fruit in turn. It will give a positive response to all of the fruits that you've handled, but will give a different response to the one that your friend handled.

Most people don't remember what day of the week their birthday falls on in the current year. This is an interesting experiment you can do with someone who either can't remember what day it was on, or hasn't yet had their birthday this year. Write the days of the week in a semicircle on a piece of paper. Ask the person to hold your pendulum halfway along the base of the semicircle. Ask: "What day of the week is your birthday on this year?" The pendulum might take a while to move, but eventually it will indicate a specific day. As virtually everyone carries a cellphone, the day the pendulum swung to can be confirmed using your phone's calendar function.

The lie detector is another popular test. The person you do it with will have to be able to use a pendulum. Ask this friend to write any number from one to ten on a piece of paper, and to place it out of sight. Tell them, "I'm going to ask you a number of questions. I'd like you to answer 'no' to each of them." Hand your pendulum to your friend and ask them to think "no." Your pendulum will produce your "no" response. Once the pendulum has started moving, ask your friend: "Did you write the number one on the piece of paper?" Your friend will reply, "No." The pendulum will continue giving the "no" response if this is correct. However, if your friend has lied, the pendulum will detect this and change its response. Allow several seconds to pass, just in case the pendulum decides to change its movement, before asking your friend if he or she wrote the number two on the piece of paper. Continue asking about each number. By the time you've asked about number ten, the pendulum will have told you what number your friend wrote down.

Some people enjoy testing themselves with a deck of cards. It's important to try this in a lighthearted manner. You should do it for both fun and practice, which means you shouldn't keep experimenting indefinitely. It's better to stop before you get bored or frustrated, no matter whether you succeed or not. There's no point in getting upset if you're not successful right away. It's better to do this for several minutes every day or two, rather than spend thirty minutes on it once a week. After the deck has been mixed, ask your pendulum if the top facedown card is, for instance, a red card. After a few successes, see if you can determine the color and the suit (hearts, diamonds, spades, or clubs). Again, once you've developed your ability at this, you might ask if the value of the card is more than seven. If you get a positive response, ask if it's an eight, nine, ten, jack, queen, or king. Your pendulum will give you a positive response when you mention the correct name of the card. If you get a negative response when you ask if the card is more than seven, ask one at a time if the card is an ace, two, three, four, five, six, and seven.

The process sounds rather drawn out, but in practice can be performed quickly, and I've met many people who are extremely good at it. However, they all developed these skills over a period of time. The more they practiced, the better they became.

Here's another experiment with playing cards. Take out the four aces, mix them, and place them facedown in a row. See if your pendulum can identify each one of them.

This experiment can be done with someone else. It's especially useful if your friend is also interested in learning how to use a pendulum. Shuffle a deck of cards and deal ten cards faceup in a row across a table. Ask your friend to mentally choose a card and focus on it. Pass your pendulum slowly over each card. The pendulum is likely to react over one of the cards, which will probably be the one your friend is focusing on. After trying this out two or three times, swap roles and give your friend a turn.

There are many experiments that can be done with playing cards. They're a useful tool, as they come in two colors, four suits, and fifty-two unique designs. This provides plenty of material for a variety of tests. Some people thrive at exercises of this sort, but they're not for everyone. If you find this type of test boring, you'll find it better to develop your skills by creating tests that are relevant to you.

You might, for instance, ask your pendulum to tell you the number of emails that have arrived since you last checked them. You might ask it to tell you how your daughter got on at the dentist this morning. Before visiting a store, you can ask if a certain item is on sale. There are all sorts of things in your daily life that you can use for dowsing practice.

In the nineteenth century, psychic experimenters found that the pendulum could tell them what the time was, even in the middle of the night when it was dark (Cosimano 1992, 57). They'd get up in the early hours of the morning, hold their pendulum close to a wall, and ask what the hour was. The pendulum would start swinging and tap the wall the necessary number of times to indicate the hour. The pendulum would tap the hours loudly, and if the time was close to the half hour, it would produce a gentle tap to indicate the half hour.

This isn't a particularly useful experiment today. However, you can use it if you're expecting a courier delivery or a repairman. Ask the pendulum what time the parcel or the person will arrive, and the pendulum will produce the required number of taps. Instead of using a wall, you might prefer to suspend your pendulum inside a drinking glass.

You'll have noticed that the element of need is lacking in all of these experiments. Once you've gained some experience with these preliminary tests, the next step is to try to find something that you've lost or can't find (see use 3 on page 43).

PART 2

50 Ways to Use a Pendulum

1: Pendulum Clearing

Pendulum clearing stimulates the flow of energy to restore balance and eliminate negative energy. This energy can be anywhere, but is commonly found in houses and people.

Negative energy can be found or created anywhere. If you're a sensitive person you might feel your stomach tightening when someone is being treated unfairly, or when you witness road rage or animal abuse. You might feel drained of energy after spending time in the company of certain people. You might be enjoying a pleasant day and suddenly be treated rudely by a stranger. All sorts of things can occur in everyday life to create negative energy that can then cause stress, anxiety, headaches, heart palpitations, and sudden changes of mood. Fortunately, your pendulum can help you eliminate these feelings and emotions.

A clearing is performed by spinning the pendulum counterclockwise (clockwise if you're left-handed) while expressing your feelings about the situation, silently or out loud, and watching the pendulum's movements until it gradually stops. Once it has, you'll know the clearing has been successful.

If you wish, you can follow this by spinning the pendulum clockwise (counterclockwise if you're left-handed) while instilling positive messages and thoughts.

General Clearing

This is a useful clearing that will enhance your life in many ways. Spin your pendulum in a counterclockwise direction and say:

> I ask (God, Universal Life Force, or whatever word you choose) to release any negativity that is adversely affecting me in any way. Please release all the negativity in my body, mind, and spirit. Please release any negativity in all the environments I find myself in today. Please also release any negativity that might be trapped inside the bodies, minds, and hearts of all the people I love. Please allow any negativity I encounter today to totally dissolve and lose any power to harm me or anyone else, in any way. Please, (Universal Life Force, Divine Spirit, God, etc.), replace all the negativity with peace, harmony, and divine love.

Think of your intent as you gaze at your pendulum until it stops moving. Once it has stopped, spin it in a clockwise direction and say:

> I ask for peace of mind, happiness, joy, and love in everything I do today. Help me spread joy and happiness everywhere I go, so that everyone I encounter will feel better as a result of my

presence. Please help me be courteous, patient, kind, and understanding, even in difficult situations. Please help me make a positive difference for everyone I encounter today.

Please strengthen my aura, so I can deflect any anxiety, stress, fear, and any other form of negativity I might encounter, yet remain open to everything that's positive and good. Please help me see the good in everyone I meet.

Please bless any food and drink I consume, and allow it to nurture my body, mind, and spirit. Please eliminate any dis-ease from my physical body, so I can enjoy radiant health and vitality. Please help me become the person I want to be. Thank you. Thank you. Thank you.

Again, watch the gyrations of your pendulum until it stops. I always say one final "thank you" when it stops moving.

Prayers and Blessings

You can use the same process that you use for a general clearing in all of your contacts with the Universal Life Force (the Divine, God, or whatever name you feel comfortable using). If you pray, for instance, see if your prayers feel enhanced if you say them while your pendulum is spinning clockwise.

Blessings are used to change people's energies. You can say blessings for yourself, but you can also perform them to help others. Whenever you can, seek someone's permission before performing a blessing on them. This isn't always possible. If someone is seriously ill in the hospital, for instance, you might need to use your own judgment.

Some people prefer to write down what they're going to say, while others like to be spontaneous and say whatever's in their mind at the time. Start by spinning your pendulum clockwise, speaking to the Universal Life Force, and asking for a blessing. Continue by asking for whatever it is you need, and finish by saying thank you. As I consider a blessing to be a form of prayer, I always finish by saying "Amen."

Here's an example of a simple blessing:

> Dear Universal Life Force, thank you for all your comfort and support. Please bless me, and all those I love. Fill me with your Divine energy to provide healing to my mind, body, and soul. Please give me all the energy I need to complete my work in this incarnation, and please provide me with opportunities to bless and help others. I am very grateful for everything you do for me. Thank you. Thank you. Thank you, Universal Life Force. Amen.

You can perform a blessing whenever you wish. First thing in the morning and just before you go to bed at night are both excellent times. If you can, perform it whenever you catch yourself thinking negative thoughts.

How to Clear Yourself before Dowsing

You need to be free of any negativity before using your pendulum. You can do this by spinning your pendulum counterclockwise while saying, "I ask the Universal Life Force to please remove all thoughts, emotions, feelings, memories, attitudes, beliefs, opinions, and anything else that could negatively affect my dowsing today. Thank you. Thank you. Thank you."

Look at your pendulum and think of your need to be free of all negativity, until the pendulum stops moving.

How to Clear Negative Entities from the Energy Field

Disincarnate energies are souls of dead people who have not moved on from the Earth plane. They attach themselves to the energy fields (auras) of people when they are unconscious, usually as a result of an accident or some other unfortunate event. If you know someone who appears to have changed personality after such an experience, the chances are that negative entities have attached themselves to him or her.

Start by asking your pendulum if the person has any negative entities in his or her energy field. If the answer is yes, continue by asking further questions to determine how many entities there are. You might start by asking: "Are there more than ten?" If the answer is yes, ask if there are more than twenty, thirty, and so on, until you receive a negative response. Then ask further questions to determine the exact number.

Ask the Universal Life Force if he or she is willing to help clear the entities. If you get a positive response you can proceed with the clearing. Spin the pendulum counter-clockwise and say:

> I ask the Universal Life Force to take all (number) of the entities that are affecting (person's name) to the dimension where they truly belong. Please remove all the negativity that has affected (person's name) as a result of having these entities in his/her energy field, and strengthen his/her aura to provide protection from any entities at any time in the future. Thank you. Thank you. Thank you.

How to Clear Negative Entities from the Home

Almost everyone has at some time experienced negative energy in a house. Often this appears to be in a specific area, but sometimes the whole house has an unpleasant, even evil, feeling. Doing a clearing to remove negative entities can make a huge difference to the emotional feel of a house. You can perform a house clearing inside the home, or wherever you happen to be. If you're not in the house, you'll need to identify it at the start of the clearing.

Spin the pendulum counterclockwise and say:

> Universal Life Force, please remove any negative entities trapped in this home and guide them to where they truly belong. Please remove all of the negative energy from this home to enable it to become a haven for peace, love, and friendship, where people can live their lives in harmony. If there is any other form of negativity affecting this home, please send it to where it belongs for the good of all. Thank you. Thank you. Thank you.

You can learn more about removing negative energies in pendulum use 35 on page 175.

2: Setting Your Intention

Your intention is your reason or purpose for using the pendulum. Usually, the intention is obvious. If you're dowsing for water, for instance, your intention is to find water. If you've lost your car keys, your intention is to find them. Setting an intention forces you to think of what you want to achieve, and helps you focus your mind on this goal while using the pendulum.

Sometimes, though, your intention may not be obvious. It can be helpful to write down exactly what you want to achieve with your intention. Let's suppose your intention is "I will become successful." As it stands, this intention is not particularly useful or helpful. Does success mean making millions of dollars? It could mean owning your own home, finishing your degree, getting a job, becoming physically fit, winning a race, finding the right partner, or even making a new friend.

Writing down exactly what you mean by success enables you to clarify it. Let's assume you've moved to a new city where you know very few people. You want to get a good job, make friends, and ultimately buy your own home. The most important immediate goal will probably be to find work. A "good job" is not specific enough either. Do you want to continue in the same career you were in before moving? Do you have useful skills that you could utilize in a different career? What sort of work do you really want to do? How much money do you want to make? How far are you prepared to commute every day? Once you've answered these and other questions about the sort of work you want to do, you can turn it into your intention. Once you've achieved this intention, you can focus on your second intention.

Recently, I met a lady who told me her sole intention is to use her pendulum to help others. This is a noble aim, but I couldn't help thinking that she'd be much more successful if she clarified exactly how she was going to help someone whenever she picked up her pendulum.

3: Finding Something That's Lost or Hidden

We've all had the experience of losing something, such as car keys or a library book, and feeling panic when we couldn't find it. In cases of this sort, there's a genuine need to find the missing object. Often, you'll know the missing item is in your home, but because you put it down absent-mindedly, you have no idea where it is. Usually, you'll notice that it's missing when you're in a hurry and need the item urgently. Most people have had this experience with their car keys.

The first step is to calm down and relax. It's almost impossible to use a pendulum when you're feeling stressed. Drink a glass of water and take several slow, deep breaths before starting to dowse.

Method One

Ask the pendulum a question that you think you know the answer to. If you've lost your car keys and think they're somewhere in your home, you might ask, "Are the car keys in the house?" If they are, your pendulum will give a positive response. This is a good start, as it allows you to now narrow the search down. It's also good news to get a negative response, as you'll know your car keys are outside, and you can ask further questions, such as "Are they in the car?" until you find them.

Continue asking questions that will lead you to the lost object. You might inquire, "Are the keys in the kitchen?" Ask questions about each room in the house until you receive a positive answer. Sometimes this is all that's necessary. Once you know what room it's in, you may recall exactly where you left it, and then be able to go to the room and pick it up. There's a phenomenon known as *remanence*, which says that everything leaves a trace memory that remains for a while after the object has been moved. This means that the missing item will at some point have been in the room the pendulum indicated, but may no longer be there. Consequently, you should also ask, "Are the keys in (the room) now?"

You have a number of choices once you know the lost object is in a particular room. You might go to the room and search it until you find the item. Alternatively, you could ask questions, such as "Is it under the bed?" or "Is it in the closet?" You could even ask about each particular drawer in a chest of drawers.

The other method is to stand in the entrance of the room with the pendulum in your hand and ask it to locate the missing object. Your pendulum will swing to indicate the direction the object is in. Move to another part of the room, and again ask your pendulum to locate the object. As before, it will swing to indicate the correct direction. You'll find the missing item where the two invisible lines intersect.

You can experiment with these methods before anything is lost. Ask a friend to hide a small object somewhere in your home. With practice, you'll be able to ask your pendulum questions that will enable you to successfully find it.

You can also stand at the entrance to a room and ask your pendulum to locate an object that you can see. The pendulum will swing to indicate the object. Once you've done that, move to another part of the room and ask the pendulum the same question. Again, the pendulum will swing in the right direction.

Another way to practice is to ask a friend to hide a coin, such as a quarter, under a rug. Slowly pass your pendulum over the rug until it responds to indicate where the coin is hidden. Many years ago, I saw Docc Hilford, a good friend of mine and an expert dowser from Arizona, perform this experiment in a hotel lobby. Five quarters were hidden under a large rug. Several people watched the experiment, and we were all surprised when Docc's pendulum successfully located seven quarters (Webster 1996, 163)!

Method Two

You can use this method if you have some idea where the missing object is. If, for instance, you know your car keys are somewhere inside your house, you can walk slowly from room to room with the pendulum suspended from your hand. Focus on your need to find the missing item. The pendulum will start to swing as you get close to the item, and will swing more and more vigorously as you get closer to it. This method is more difficult than the first method, as you need to be finely attuned to the movements of your pendulum.

Method Three

If you know the missing object is somewhere in your home, you can stand at your front door with your pendulum in your hand. Visualize the missing object. Your pendulum will start to swing in the direction you can move to find the lost object. Walk slowly in that direction, pausing every now and again to make sure the pendulum hasn't changed its movement. Follow the indications of the pendulum until it stops moving or starts revolving in a circle. Your missing item should be at this point.

Methods two and three are useful when you're trying to find something that's been mislaid. However, there will be times when you're trying to find something that has been completely lost, and no one has any idea where it might be. If you have mislaid something, your subconscious mind will provide you with the necessary information to find it. If the item is totally lost, your pendulum will obtain the necessary information from the Universal Mind.

I once observed a farmer find a lost lamb. He stood on the highest point of his farm with his pendulum in his right hand. He extended his left arm and hand and slowly turned 360 degrees. At one point, his pendulum started gyrating. He started walking in the direction the pendulum had indicated, stopping every two or three minutes to check that he was still going in the right direction. After walking for about twenty minutes, he found the lamb, apparently perfectly happy, beside a small stream.

After Abbé Mermet had given a lecture on the pendulum, a doctor asked Mermet if he would try an experiment in his presence. The doctor was accompanied by a small girl and her mother. The girl had swallowed a button and the doctor and mother wanted to know if it was still in her body. The priest used his pendulum and told the doctor exactly where the button was located in her body. A few days later, Mermet received a message from the doctor saying, "The little girl has been X-rayed and the place you indicated was quite correct" (Mermet 1959, 99). In this instance, no one knew where the button was, but Mermet was able to find it using his pendulum.

4. Making Your Dreams a Reality

We all have hopes, dreams, and desires. Thanks to our creative minds, we have the ability to turn these ideas into reality. Sadly, few people reach the levels of success that they truly could achieve. There are many reasons for this. Fear, doubt, and worry are the main ones.

There are five steps to turn your dreams into reality. The first is to create an intention. The second step is to believe that you can achieve this goal. The third is to express gratitude to the universe for enabling it to manifest. The fourth step is to make a plan to achieve your goal; the fifth and final step is to do whatever is necessary to make it a reality.

Step One: Create Your Intention

As this involves turning a dream into reality, you need to choose a worthwhile goal. Ideally, it should be something that you initially think might be beyond your reach. Spend time working out exactly what it is you desire, and then write it down on paper. Ask your pendulum if this goal is something you really want. If you get a positive response you can move on to the second step. With any other response, you need to ask further questions to decide what to do. You might ask, "Is there something better for me that I should ask for?" You can follow this up with further questions to help you decide what to do next. Another question you should ask is "Would realizing this goal be beneficial for me?"

If you have a number of possible intentions, you should write them down on separate sheets of paper and suspend your pendulum over each question in turn, asking, "Is this the intention I should pursue now?" Doing this will tell you which intention you should focus on, and you can ask your pendulum if it's something you really want. Your intention must be something that you really want, as you'll be putting a great deal of time and effort into achieving it. I've met many people who've worked hard to fulfil parental expectations, but gained little or no satisfaction from doing so. The satisfaction of success comes when you achieve a worthwhile goal that you set for yourself, and make it happen.

Step Two: Belief

You must believe that you can achieve your goal. It's all very well setting an intention, but if, deep down, you don't believe you can attain it, you won't be successful. Sit down with your pendulum, relax, and close your eyes. Think about your intention. Visualize it as clearly as possible in your mind. See yourself in different situations once your dream has become a reality. Feel how happy you are to have achieved this goal. Focus on these thoughts for as long as you can. When you feel ready, say, out loud or silently, "I believe I can achieve this dream. I'm prepared to do whatever it takes to make this dream a reality. I can do this. I have the ability to achieve anything I wish, and this goal will make a huge difference to my life. I know I will achieve this goal. I believe, I believe, I believe." Open your eyes and see what movement your pendulum is making. If it's saying yes, you can move on to step three. If not, you have further work to do before you can start manifesting this goal.

Belief is vital. Without belief you'll sabotage yourself and the dream will never come to be. Fortunately, you can build up your belief by constantly thinking of your goal and affirming to yourself that you can, and will, achieve it. Use your pendulum to measure your belief every day until it says yes. Only then can you move on to step three.

Step Three: Express Gratitude

You need to start expressing your gratitude to the universe as soon as you reach this step. Give thanks, and feel grateful for the wonderful gift the universe is giving you. Once a day, sit down with your pendulum, spin it clockwise, and give thanks to the universe until the pendulum stops moving. As well as giving thanks, feel yourself in possession of your desire, and visualize yourself as you'll be once it has appeared. Continue giving thanks with your pendulum every day until you've achieved your intention. In addition to this, silently give thanks whenever you have a spare moment. Allow yourself to feel the joy and the emotions you'll experience once the goal becomes a reality.

Step Four: Make a Plan

You now know that your desire is attainable. However, it's unlikely to come to fruition without planning and hard work. Take time to work out a step-by-step plan that will lead you to your goal. Use your pendulum to advise you about every step.

Step Five: Take Action

Once your plan has been made, start working on the first step right away. It doesn't matter how small it is. Nothing can happen until you take that vital first step. Once you achieve that, start on the second step of your plan, and continue following your plan until you reach your goal. Express your gratitude (step three) every day while you're working on achieving your intention.

5. The Pendulum and Your Career

It would be impossible to estimate the number of people who dislike, or even hate, their work. Many people fall into careers virtually by accident. They might accept the first job they're offered, as it is, after all, a job. Others go into certain careers to fulfill parental expectations. A close relative of mine chose his career solely because it paid well. It didn't take him long to discover that it was the wrong way to choose a career, and he's now working in a field that he loves instead.

Other, more fortunate people know at an early age what they want to do. My father always wanted to be a doctor, worked hard, and became one. He didn't need to think about a suitable career, as he always knew what he wanted to do. Most people aren't like that. Fortunately, the humble pendulum is able to help these unsure people discover what they should be doing in this incarnation.

In fact, your pendulum can help you at every stage in your career. If you're about to enter the work force you can ask your pendulum for advice on the type of career you'd most enjoy doing, and then gradually narrow it down to a particular corporation by asking, "Is this the best company for me to work in?" or "Will I be happy working there?"

You might have a degree, but have no idea how to make the best use of it. Before focusing on a particular career, you should ask: "Is this the best career for me?"; "Will I be happy in this career?"; and "Will I be successful in this career?"

I know several people who've chosen the right careers for themselves by making a list of all their hobbies and interests, and then asking their pendulums to indicate which of these could be turned into a satisfying and fulfilling career.

One woman I know is now a preschool teacher. She spent ten unhappy years working in an insurance company doing work that she found mind-numbingly dull and uninteresting. She'd never thought of working with children until her pendulum told her it would be a good career move.

The best mechanic I know always wanted to work with cars, but became a school teacher, as his parents considered it a more prestigious career than working with his hands. He enjoyed teaching, but it was never a passion. His pendulum told him what he always knew, and even though it caused considerable hardship at the time, he changed careers. He now owns his own shop and is extremely happy.

Once you've found a suitable position, you can monitor your progress with your pendulum. Ask it questions about your career on a regular basis. For example:

- Is my supervisor happy with my work?

- Is this a good time to ask for a raise?

- Should I change jobs?

• Should I change my career?

• Is this report good enough to submit to my boss?

You'll be offered a number of opportunities as you progress in your career, and will be able to assess them with the help of your pendulum. You might ask, "Is this a worthwhile opportunity?" or "Will this opportunity help me reach my goals?"

No matter what type of work you choose, the chances are high that from time to time you'll be called upon to make decisions. Some of these are likely to be important decisions.

A friend of mine used to be the buyer for a large mail order company, and dealt with companies all around the world. She regularly used her pendulum when deciding which items, and in what quantity, she needed to order.

Not long ago, I needed an artist to illustrate a project I was working on. Several people applied, but two were noticeably better than the rest. I used my pendulum to help me decide which one to employ.

Your pendulum will be just as useful if you have the opportunity to start or buy a business. You can ask if the price you're paying is fair, if you'll be able to borrow any money you may require to buy it, if the business will be successful, if you'll enjoy being self-employed, if the people closest to you will be supportive, and anything else that's relevant to your situation.

6. Meditating with a Pendulum

Meditation is the act of entering a state in which the mind is calm and relaxed, and your energies are either diffused or focused on a single idea. Meditation gives you the opportunity to get beyond your mind and find your true spiritual nature deep within. Dowsing with a pendulum is a form of meditation. Meditation is an effective way to gain insight and find inner peace, harmony, compassion, love, and a sense of the inter-connectedness of all living things.

Your pendulum will help you relax and get into the desired meditative state. Think of something pleasant, such as someone you love or a beautiful scene, and watch the pendulum move in your positive direction. Allow your breathing to follow the movements of your pendulum, and continue thinking positive thoughts until you feel fully relaxed.

Your pendulum can help with every aspect of your meditation. You can, for instance, ask your pendulum how long you should meditate for today. You do this by asking the pendulum if you can meditate for a modest length of time of your choosing. If the response if positive, ask the question again but increase the length of time by five or ten minutes. Continue doing this until you get a negative response. This will tell you the optimum length of time you can spend meditating today.

Incidentally, you don't need to meditate for long to receive significant benefits. An article in *Psychology Today* said that meditating for ten minutes will produce dramatic effects, such as "increased alpha waves (the relaxed brain waves) and decreased anxiety and depression" (Barbor 2001).

Here's a short pendulum meditation that many people have found helpful. All you need is a comfortable armchair in a place where you won't be disturbed for about fifteen minutes, and your pendulum.

Sit down in the armchair. If you're right-handed, rest your right elbow on the arm of this chair and hold the pendulum in your right hand. (If you're left-handed, use your left elbow and hand.) Ask your pendulum if you can meditate on a particular goal or concern. If you receive a positive response to this, you can proceed.

Take several slow, deep breaths, and relax as much as you can. Think of happy moments from the past, and watch your pendulum produce your positive response. Take three more deep breaths, and say to yourself, "relax, relax, relax" each time you exhale. When you feel reasonably relaxed, start thinking about your goal. If you wish to eliminate a problem or concern from your life, swing your pendulum in a counterclockwise direction. Gaze at your pendulum while it's revolving and think about your concern and what your life will be like once the problem has been resolved. Remain detached and as unemotional as possible while the pendulum is circling. As the pendulum slows down, give thanks to the universe for helping you release the concern from your mind. Continue thinking along this line until the pendulum comes to a stop.

If your desire is to attract something worthwhile into your life, spin your pendulum in a clockwise direction and think positive thoughts about your goal until the pendulum slows down and stops. Remember to give thanks to the universe for bringing this blessing into your life, while the pendulum is still circling.

Pause and think of the special people in your life. If you wish, close your eyes to visualize them clearly in your mind. When you're ready, swing the pendulum clockwise again and, as you watch it circling, send peace, harmony, and love to all the people you visualized. Thank the universe for bringing them into your life. As the pendulum comes to a stop, say, "Thank you. Thank you. Thank you."

Stay in this quiet, meditative state for as long as you wish. When you feel ready, take three slow, deep breaths and get up. Have a drink of water and eat a few nuts or raisins before continuing with your day.

When you start meditating, you're likely to find it hard to remain focused on your goal, as random thoughts will come into your mind. Don't try to stop them. Simply be aware of them, and let them come and go as they wish. Return to your meditation when you're ready.

Some people feel that meditations should always be done with the eyes closed. In fact, *dzogchen*, the highest form of Tibetan Buddhist meditation, is done with the eyes open. In the above meditation you can open and close your eyes whenever you wish. You might want to open your eyes every now and then to check on your pendulum's movements, and then close them again.

This pendulum meditation is my favorite form of meditation.

7. The Pendulum and Self-Improvement

Hopefully, we continue growing and developing all the way through our lives. Many people set resolutions or goals for themselves at the start of each year. These are hopes and wishes that people set with the intention of improving their lives in some way. Sadly, most of these New Year's resolutions are quickly forgotten, usually in a matter of days.

There are many reasons for this. The goal might have been an idle thought or daydream that the person didn't expect to accomplish. The goal might have been set to please others. Goals of this sort are incredibly hard to achieve. The right goal is one that is realistic, and one that you are prepared to do whatever is necessary to achieve. The pendulum can tell you if you're willing to do all the things that are required to reach your goal.

It can be a revealing exercise to hold your pendulum and repeat your goal several times. A positive response shows that your subconscious mind accepts the goal and will help you to accomplish it. However, if you receive a negative response, you'll need to ask further questions to find out if this goal is something you really, really want.

Let's assume that you're thinking of returning to college to complete your degree. It's been several years since you did any serious study, and you now have a partner and children. You're working long hours to make ends meet. Is completing your degree a silly idea given your current situation? For many people, it probably is. However, I've met many people over the years who have achieved worthwhile goals despite having plenty of reasons why they shouldn't. Why can some people do this, while others can't? The reason is that the goal is so important for these people that they find the necessary motivation, energy, and persistence to achieve it.

If you have a self-improvement goal in mind, you can ask your pendulum if you're prepared to do whatever is necessary to achieve it. In fact, you can ask as many questions as you wish about the goal. If the goal is the right one for you, your pendulum will let you know.

Your pendulum can advise you on what books to read and study. I've read many books that I would have overlooked if I hadn't asked my pendulum about them.

When my younger son was a teenager, he decided to join a gym. He visited several and couldn't decide which one would be best for him. We asked my pendulum which gym he should choose, based on the outcomes he wanted. To our surprise, the pendulum told us the second cheapest gym would be the best. This proved to be the case, and he remained a member until he moved overseas several years later.

Self-Assessment

It's a highly revealing process to assess your current situation with a pendulum, and you may not be happy with some of the answers you receive. However, it's an important exercise as it helps you discover areas of your life that need to be worked on.

Sit down comfortably in a quiet space where you won't be interrupted. Say the following statements out loud, and then check to see what response your pendulum gives. I prefer to close my eyes while saying each statement. I then wait several seconds before opening my eyes to see what response my pendulum is making. The pendulum will move in a positive direction if it agrees with what you've said. In the same way, it will move in a negative direction if your subconscious mind disagrees. You may find that your pendulum makes no response at all to some of the statements. This means it doesn't feel particularly strongly about what you've said, or is unsure of the answer. Record the responses you receive and repeat the exercise regularly. Over a period of time, this will provide a valuable indication of how you are progressing.

Here are the statements:

- I am happy.

- I am loved.

- I am a good person.

- I am succeeding in (life, or whatever it happens to be).

- I am following my heart's desire.

- I deserve to be successful.

- I deserve all the good things life has to offer.

- I enjoy excellent health.

- I am positive.

- I am enthusiastic.

- I am confident.

- I achieve my goals.

- I attract good things to me.

- I am free from stress.

Add any other statements that relate to your life. You might say "I am a good parent" or "I have a happy marriage." Naturally, you'd only say those things if you were married or had children.

Try not to think about the responses as you record them. I find it best to quickly move on to the next statement to prevent myself from querying about what the pendulum indicated. Once you've completed the assessment, look at the answers, especially the negative ones. Some of these may be what you expected, but others may surprise you. Ask your pendulum further questions to find out why it gave you the responses it did. Once you've discovered what the underlying reasons are, you can start working on rectifying the problem or situation.

Eliminating Bad Habits

Habits can be hard to change. This is because we're trying to change long-standing patterns of behavior using nothing but willpower. Fortunately, your pendulum can help you discover what the feelings behind these patterns of behavior are. Once you know what they are, you can let them go and replace them with positive new habits.

This can be done with any habit, such as smoking, overeating, procrastinating, gambling, or overspending. Ask your pendulum to help you achieve your goal, and see what response it gives you.

If you receive a positive response, you can then ask your pendulum about different things you can do to achieve your goal. If the goal is to lose twenty-five pounds, for instance, you could ask your pendulum for advice on exercise and food. If you receive a negative response, you need to find out why your pendulum won't help you. Once you've uncovered this, your pendulum will be more than happy to help you.

8. Eliminating Fears, Doubts, and Worries

Everyone experiences fear, doubt, and worry at different times. Way back in mankind's early history, fear was a useful quality, as people were surrounded by threats to their lives virtually all the time. It's still a useful trait today, as it can help you run for your life or take other evasive action when you're being threatened or attacked. Fortunately, that's likely to be a rare occurrence as long as you avoid potentially dangerous people and situations.

Sadly, many people live in a constant state of anxiety, insecurity, despair, and hopelessness because they feel unable to release their fears, doubts, and worries.

Fear, doubt, and worry start making themselves apparent when you step out of your comfort zone. It shows you that you no longer feel safe and protected. However, if you want to grow and develop as a person, you need to release these feelings and deliberately move out of your comfortable space. If fear holds you back from doing this, you'll never become the person you were born to be.

Worry also holds people back. Everyone has worries. People agonize over money, relationships, work, health, and a huge variety of other things.

Fortunately, your pendulum can help you with this. Spin your pendulum counterclockwise and ask it to eliminate all the fears, doubts, and worries that are holding you back. Gaze at your pendulum and think about all the lost opportunities and experiences you missed because of your concerns. Thank your pendulum for removing them from your life.

When the pendulum stops moving, stand up and move around for a few minutes. Take some deep breaths and think about how wonderful your life will be when you're free from all the self-destructive negative thoughts and emotions that have slowed you down.

When you feel ready, spin your pendulum in a clockwise direction and ask it to help you attract all that is good and positive into your life. Think of some specific things you'll be able to do now that you're free of all the fears and doubts and worries that held you back. Thank your pendulum for attracting so much positivity into your life. Continue doing this until the pendulum comes to a stop.

Over the next few days, do your best to keep track of your thoughts. Whenever you find yourself thinking or saying anything negative, stop immediately, then see if you can turn the thought around and make it positive.

Repeat the ritual as often as necessary until the negativity has completely gone.

9. Understanding Others

Empathy is the ability to visualize oneself in someone else's position and sense their thoughts and feelings. The ability to empathize has been described as "the building block of our sociality and morality" (Iacoboni 2009). Empathetic people are sensitive to others. They listen carefully and pick up cues from a person's tone of voice, expressions, and body language.

Some people are naturally empathetic, but it's a skill that anyone can develop. For instance, if you saw someone fall over and graze their knee, you'd probably wince, as for a moment you'd be feeling what the other person was experiencing. Almost everyone would react in that way, showing that most people possess empathy.

You can increase your empathy by paying attention to your own feelings and emotions. If you understand your own feelings, you're much more likely to be able to sense the feelings of others.

Listen carefully when other people are speaking. In *Across the River and into the Trees*, Ernest Hemingway said, "When people talk, listen completely. Most people never listen." It's good advice. Whatever someone talks about is important to him or her. Consequently, try to sense what people are saying from their point of view. Even someone who is boring you can become interesting when you try to understand what they are saying, from their point of view.

We all have feelings, and most of us are much more sensitive than we let on. If you pay attention to people's feelings and react to them with kindness and compassion, you'll be acting empathetically.

Your pendulum is a valuable tool that can help you understand and get along with others. Before meeting someone, swing your pendulum in a positive direction and send thoughts of empathy and warmth to the person you're going to see. You'll find your interaction will get off to a much better start when you do this. You'll go into the meeting feeling friendly and positive, and your attitude will make the other person feel good too. The chances are high that the other person will have picked up your pendulum message and will be looking forward to the meeting too.

If the person you're going to meet is someone you don't get along well with, you might choose to start the ritual by swinging the pendulum in a counterclockwise direction to release your negative feelings about the person. When the pendulum stops moving, swing it in a positive direction and send good thoughts to the universe about this person. If you do this, you'll notice a subtle change when you see each other. You'll feel more relaxed, the meeting will be more harmonious, and you and the other person will communicate more effectively and empathetically with each other.

If you're having problems with anyone, you can ask your pendulum questions about him or her, and find out what you can do to improve the relationship. You should finish by swinging your pendulum in a clockwise direction to send positive thoughts to the person.

10. The Pendulum and Character Analysis

We all pride ourselves on being good judges of character. This isn't surprising, as we've been reading people's characters since we were babies. We quickly learned to divide adults and other children into categories of "good" or "bad," and were able to use this knowledge to get along with others. As adults, our skills of judging people's characters makes life smoother and easier. However, no matter how good we think we are at character analysis, every now and again we'll be fooled by someone who proves not to be the good, honest, upright person we'd believed they were.

We tend to judge people quickly, and make assessments such as, "I don't like the look of him" or "He seems like a good person." It can take months to discover that the person who didn't appeal to us at first sight is actually an extremely likeable and ethical person. Similarly, the person we liked on first meeting might turn out to be dishonest and sly.

When we meet someone for the first time, we subliminally pick up a great deal of information about him or her. We notice the person's body language, facial expressions, tone of voice, and emotional energy in a matter of seconds. Our intuition immediately tells us whether or not we can trust this person. However, as we can't rely entirely on first impressions, it's useful to have an instrument that will happily answer any questions you may have about the person.

You can ask your pendulum about anyone you meet. With experience, you'll be able to determine someone's character by holding your pendulum over a photograph of the person, their date of birth, or their name. It makes no difference if the person is alive or dead, and it can be an interesting and useful exercise to determine the characters of famous historical figures.

While doing this, I usually ask questions along the lines of these:

- Is (name of person) honorable?

- Is (name) honest?

- Would I enjoy spending time with (name)?

- Is (name) someone I'd like to be friends with?

- Will I ever get close to (name)?

- Is (name) a good worker?

- Would I work well with (name)?

- Are they extroverted?

- Are they introverted?

- Are they emotionally stable?

- Are they a deep thinker?

- Are they quiet?

- Are they outgoing?

- Are they shy?

- Are they patient?

- Can I trust them?

You can ask as many questions as you wish, depending on what you want to know about this person. Many years ago, I met someone who used her pendulum to determine the IQs of people she considered dating. She wrote numbers, starting with eighty, eighty-five, and ninety, up to two hundred, on a sheet of paper, and then held her pendulum over each number in turn, asking it, "Is this (the person's) IQ?" Her pendulum gave a positive response when she was over the right number. I'm sure she asked other questions about potential dates, too, but this is the one I remember, as it seemed a strange thing to ask before even meeting the person.

You can use your pendulum as a lie detector too. Hold your pendulum and ask it to let you know when someone tells a lie. It will respond accordingly. The movement will be slight if the fib is a minor one, and vigorous if the lie is a major falsification. This can be an entertaining, though disillusioning, exercise if you do it while watching politicians on television.

You probably won't want to hold your pendulum while having a conversation with someone you don't trust. Instead, you might use body dowsing (see appendix), or wait until you're on your own and can ask your pendulum if the person was telling you the truth. You need to be careful when doing this, as you have the ability to overrule what your pendulum wants to say. If you think the person was lying, your pendulum will give you the answer you want, rather than the correct answer, which may be quite different.

11. The Pendulum and Your Future

Virtually everyone is curious about the future and what it will bring. Fortune-telling is still as popular as ever because people want to part the veil and see if the future will bring them a loving relationship, good health, and enough money to lead a happy and fulfilling life.

The pendulum is a useful tool to determine what lies ahead. However, because we have free will, we have the ability to change our futures. Consequently, what the pendulum indicates today may not necessarily be the outcome five years from now. What it will reveal is the most likely outcome based on the current situation. If the situation changes, the prediction will no longer be valid. I know many people who have completely turned their lives around, and as a result, changed their entire future.

A good friend of mine is a highly successful motivational speaker. Thirty years ago, he was a car thief who made his living by stealing expensive cars to order. Eventually, he got caught. While in prison, he listened as other inmates swore that they'd never return. He noticed that most of them did. He decided that would not happen to him. He was dyslexic, and learned to read and write while in prison. When he was released, he went to college and completed a degree. He then became a successful sportsman, entrepreneur, and speaker. If someone had asked a pendulum about his future before he went to prison, I'm sure the prediction would not have indicated the successful career he's had since then.

Another problem is that we have the ability to influence the movements of the pendulum. The usual suggestion is to ask someone who has no interest in the outcome to ask the question for you. This is not always practical, but fortunately, there is another method that can be used.

Write the four possible answers your pendulum can make on pieces of paper, and place them inside envelopes. Mix the envelopes thoroughly, until you can no longer tell where any of the answers are. Ask your question, trying to remain as detached from the outcome as possible, while holding your pendulum over each of the envelopes in turn. The answer will be inside the envelope it indicates.

You might not be able to receive specific answers about the future, but you can determine the chances of success in any situation. You can do this using a pendulum chart that shows you the chances of success in the form of a percentage.

Future Time

Your pendulum can be used to predict the time a certain event will occur. If, for instance, you're intending to replace your car, you can ask your pendulum to indicate when that will happen. It can measure the time in hours, days, weeks, months, or even years. You can do this by asking your pendulum a series of questions. Alternately, you can suspend your pendulum inside a glass and ask it how many weeks (or whatever period of time you wish) it will take to find the car you desire at a price you can afford. The pendulum will start moving and will tap the side of the glass a number of times to indicate the length of time.

My mother told me that her grandmother used this method to determine when visitors would arrive. She knew people would be paying her a visit on a particular day, but with no phones or any other way to contact them back then, she used her pendulum to tell her what time she had to be ready to greet them. I assume she determined the hour first, and then asked for the number of minutes.

You can also use your pendulum to part the veil and gain glimpses of the future. See use 25 on page 131.

12. Love and Compatibility

Love is, by far, the most important human emotion. Unfortunately, it's also the most complex. Without exception, everyone wants to be loved, but it's not always easy. Some people meet the right person and fall in love when they're young, while others spend a large portion of their lives trying to find the right relationship for them.

Before becoming emotionally involved with someone, you can save a great deal of time by asking your pendulum if the person likes you. Use a photograph of him or her, if you have one. If you don't, write their name on a piece of paper. Hold your pendulum over the photograph or name. Your pendulum will produce your positive response if the person likes you. Naturally, it will give a negative response if they don't.

Of course, if you have an emotional involvement in the outcome, your pendulum will give you the response you want. In that case, you should ask someone who is not emotionally involved to use the pendulum for you. You might write a list of six to ten people, one of which is the person you're interested in. Before leaving the room, ask your friend to hold the pendulum over each name for about ten seconds before moving on to the next, and make a note of the responses it gives over each name.

Your pendulum can provide useful advice on all matters relating to love and compatibility. You can, for instance, ask your pendulum when you'll meet the right person for you. You can also ask questions about a potential partner before meeting them. You could ask, "Is he/she a sincere and honorable person?" If someone asks you out, it would be a good idea to ask, "Should I go on this date?" After more dates, you might ask, "Is this going to be a good relationship for me?"; "Are we compatible?"; "Does he/she love me?"; and "Is he/she my soulmate?" You can continue asking your pendulum questions about your relationship indefinitely. Of course, if the relationship isn't going anywhere, you can also ask your pendulum if you should end it.

If you're in the fortunate position of having two or more people interested in you, your pendulum can help you determine which one would be the best choice. You'll need a number of cards about the size of a business card. Write your name on one of these. Write the names of the other people on different cards.

Place the card with your name on it in front of you, and place one of the other cards a few inches away. Suspend your pendulum between the two cards and ask it if these two people are compatible. Your pendulum will respond. It may swing from one card to the other, or it may give your positive response if you're compatible and your negative response if you aren't. Alternatively, it might rotate clockwise to indicate that you're compatible, and counterclockwise if you aren't. Repeat this with the other cards.

After doing this, hold your pendulum over the card that has the name of the person you're potentially interested in, and ask if they would be happy in a relationship with you. This time you'll receive either a positive or negative response.

Repeat this experiment with the names you wrote on the other cards. If the pendulum says that you're compatible with more than one of the people, you can measure the strength of this compatibility by using a pendulum chart to see which of them has the highest reading.

You can gain further information by asking the pendulum to assess the other person's mental, physical, emotional, and spiritual compatibility with you. Obviously, it's extremely good if there's compatibility on all four levels. If there's a good rating on the physical level, the two people will get on well sexually. They'll enjoy a good love affair if the emotional rating is high, too. If the mental level is also high, there is a strong potential for a long-lasting relationship. This is enhanced further with a good spiritual compatibility, which means the two people share similar spiritual ideals.

You can also use your pendulum to send love to others. Spin your pendulum clockwise and send thoughts of love to the person you have in mind. Continue thinking about this person, and send loving thoughts to them until the pendulum stops.

You're not restricted to individual people, either. You can send love to all humanity. You can also send love to a favorite pet or other animal. You can send love to your spirit guides and angel guardians. A friend of mine regularly sends love to an old oak tree that she's adored since childhood.

You can send love to anyone. You might send love to your Facebook friends, your dentist, or the person sitting opposite you on a bus or train. While you're sending love to others, you should also send it to people you don't like. Over a period of time you'll find that your relationship with these people will improve. They may not know what you're doing, but they'll subliminally sense and respond to your messages of love.

Most importantly of all, you should regularly send love to yourself. You'll appreciate all the blessings in your life much more as a result. You'll value yourself more. Your self-esteem will be strong and healthy. You'll enjoy better relationships with everyone, and will be better able to withstand any adversity that comes your way.

13. The Pendulum and Travel

A friend of mine inherited some money and decided to spend it on a vacation in Bali. All her friends encouraged her to go. However, she'd never traveled internationally, and was nervous about traveling on her own. Despite talking about it endlessly, it began to look as if the idea of travel was simply an idle thought and would never happen. Kath owned a pendulum, and I suggested that she ask it for advice about whether or not she should travel, and when to do it if she did decide to go.

Kath took my idea much further than I'd suggested. She asked a series of questions about every aspect of the trip. Her pendulum told her that travel would be good for her, and that she would thoroughly enjoy it. It told her that she'd be perfectly happy traveling on her own, but would enjoy it more if she went with a friend. Kath asked the pendulum about different friends, and narrowed it down to one. This person was also single, and was delighted to be asked if she'd like to come, as she didn't like the idea of traveling on her own either. Now that Kath had someone to travel with, she started asking her pendulum about different places they could go. The pendulum suggested they visit Singapore and Kuala Lumpur as well as Bali.

Kath then dowsed for the best time of year to travel, the best airline, suitable places to stay in each destination, and what they should see and do in each place.

Thanks to her pendulum, Kath and her friend had a wonderful vacation, and have traveled together several times since. Without it, she would probably still be thinking about traveling one day.

Your pendulum will prove invaluable whenever you want or need to travel anywhere. It will answer all your questions, small or large, and will remove much of the stress and anxiety that travel can create.

Travel delays and flight cancellations are common nowadays, and you can ask your pendulum about the likelihood of these occurring. This gives you the opportunity to make alternative plans if necessary.

If you travel on business, you can ask your pendulum if it would be beneficial to visit a certain customer on a particular date. You can ask if the person or people you're going to see will have time to see you. You might save time if you ask if it would be more beneficial to phone the customer, rather than travel to see them.

14. Revealing and Understanding Your Hidden Fears

The pendulum is a highly effective way to gain information from your subconscious mind. Most people are subliminally influenced by false beliefs and fears that hold them back and prevent them from developing their true potential. It could be a fear of rejection, fear of what others may think, fear of failure, fear of being unworthy, fear of uncertainty, fear of abandonment, fear of being unlovable, or almost any other deep-seated fear. I know a man who wanted to start his own business, but never did because of his fear of failure. I've worked with many people who had a fear of being rejected when cold calling over the phone. Many of these fears date back to childhood, and no longer have any relevance to the person in the present. The frustration and anger this fear creates prevent the person from ever feeling truly happy. It can, in extreme cases, totally ruin the person's life.

Fortunately, you can eliminate any hidden fears and anxieties you have with the help of your pendulum. If you wish, you can even do this without having to know what these hidden fears are.

Ask your pendulum if it will help you connect with your subconscious mind. If you receive a positive answer, ask your pendulum if you're harboring any hidden fears. Most people are, so the chances are you'll receive a positive response to this question. If you receive a negative reply, you can conclude the exercise by spinning your pendulum clockwise and expressing your thanks to the universe for blessing you with such a good and positive life. If you receive a positive answer to step two, you can continue by saying, "I ask my higher self to examine my subconscious mind and remove any false beliefs about (whatever it happens to be)."

Perform a clearing by spinning your pendulum counterclockwise while thinking about whatever it is you wish to eliminate. As the pendulum slows down, thank it for helping you resolve this problem or concern. Wait until the pendulum stops. Thank it again, preferably out loud. Spin the pendulum in a clockwise circle and ask your subconscious mind to fill up the space created by your false beliefs with good, positive beliefs about yourself, your life, and the world you live in. Again, thank it as it starts slowing down.

Check on your work by asking your pendulum if you still hold any false beliefs related to this hidden fear. You should receive a negative response. If so, thank your pendulum and finish the session. If you receive a positive response, you'll need to repeat the exercise as many times as needed for your pendulum to give you a negative answer to this question.

If you wish, you can identify your hidden feelings before eliminating them. You can often identify them by the words you use. If you frequently say "what if …"; "should I …"; "I'm no good at …"; "I'll probably make a fool of myself"; or

"What's the point? No one listens to me anyway," chances are that what follows these words will reveal a hidden fear.

Once you've identified a limiting idea or feeling, you can eliminate it by spinning your pendulum counterclockwise while telling the hidden fear that you're letting it go. If possible, follow this exercise by swinging your pendulum clockwise while thinking or saying positive thoughts that are totally opposite to the old belief. Let's assume, for instance, that you avoid playing sports because of a fear of making a fool of yourself. After eliminating that old belief, you could spin your pendulum clockwise while thinking about how much you love playing the game. As the pendulum continues to spin, visualize yourself being successful at the game, and see yourself being congratulated for your skill at it.

15. The Pendulum and Shopping

I know a number of people who use their pendulums more often for shopping than for any other purpose. On a few occasions, I've seen people choosing fruit and vegetables in the supermarket by suspending their pendulums over them. I assume they're searching for produce that is free of chemicals or pesticides.

I usually have a pendulum with me when I'm shopping, but am more likely to use it before heading out to the stores. It can save a great deal of time to find out which stores have stock of whatever it is I want, at a price I'm prepared to pay. When buying online, I can determine the reputation and honesty of the company I'm planning to buy from. I can also find out how long it will take for the item to reach me, and ask any other questions that relate to my potential purchase. This is particularly important when buying from suppliers in other countries.

You can do exactly the same when shopping for services. A friend of mine recently moved to a new city and chose her new dentist by making a list of all the dentists within a ten-mile radius of her home. She held her pendulum over each name in turn, and asked a series of questions to determine which one to visit. She's very happy with the dentist her pendulum chose.

When vegetarian friends come to stay, we choose suitable restaurants to visit in the same way. Another friend suffers from severe allergies, and she chooses restaurants using her pendulum. Online, or when she's at the restaurant, she'll suspend the pendulum over any item in the menu that she's thinking of ordering to make sure that it's free of anything she's allergic to.

I'm fortunate to have a good crystal shop about fifteen miles from my home. On one occasion, I was about to drive there to buy a piece of tourmaline, when it occurred to me to ask my pendulum if they had what I wanted in stock. They didn't, which means my pendulum saved me at least an hour of time, and probably some money too, as I rarely visit the store without making a few impulse purchases.

That can be important too. It's a good idea to ask your pendulum if you really need the item you're planning to buy. Sometimes, usually if the item is a book, I'll buy it anyway, but at least I'll know who to blame if I suffer from buyer's remorse later.

16. The Pendulum and Your Car

More than twenty years ago, I used a pendulum to find a good mechanic. He has serviced my car ever since. When a friend of mine was thinking of replacing his car several years ago, he held his pendulum over advertisements in the daily paper, and asked his pendulum questions about the cars that sounded interesting. The pendulum gave a positive response over six of them, and ultimately told him which one he should buy. If he were to do that today, he'd probably do his search online, but the process would be exactly the same.

You can save a great deal of money by asking your pendulum questions about your car before taking it in for a service. This can be extremely useful if you're aware of a problem, but don't know exactly what it is. By asking a series of questions, you can pinpoint the location of the problem, and then find out exactly what is causing it to happen.

You can also use your pendulum to check what your mechanic tells you. If you know little about cars, and your mechanic tells you your car needs a new transmission, you can ask your pendulum if a new transmission is actually necessary.

Some years ago, I stopped to help a man who was parked on the side of the road with his hood open. When I got close, I saw that he was using a pendulum to find out what was wrong. I introduced myself by saying that I used a pendulum, too. A few moments later, his pendulum indicated a loose connection, and he was able to make a temporary repair. He was a farmer, and before I left him, he told me that the pendulum was his "secret tool" that he used to solve "any and every" problem he encountered.

If you ever find yourself broken down on the side of the road, hold your pendulum over the engine and slowly move it until you get a response. A counterclockwise movement, or your negative response, will tell you what part of the engine has caused the problem. Once you know that, you can ask further questions to find out exactly what the fault is.

Fortunately, I've never been in that situation, but it's comforting to know that I have a "secret tool" that can help me if my car ever breaks down when I'm far from home.

17. Using Your Pendulum as Your Elixir of Life

The elixir of life was a legendary liquid that gave the drinker eternal life or eternal youth. The origin of this legend dates back thousands of years to when Chinese emperors sought it, and it appears in different forms in most cultures. Today the phrase "elixir of life" relates to anything that keeps a person energetic and young in heart and spirit.

Life is much more enjoyable when you're young at heart. The fact that you're reading a book on pendulums shows that you possess a great deal of curiosity and enjoy exploring different activities. This shows that, no matter how old you may be—or will become—in physical years, you'll always have a youthful approach to life.

There are many other ways to stay young at heart. Socialize with positive people, be spontaneous, laugh frequently, do something you really enjoy every day, and make sure you always have something exciting to look forward to. Spend time with younger people, and see the world from their point of view. Keep up-to-date with what's going on in the world. Learn something new. Visit new places—travel is a wonderful way to meet new people, see exotic places, and keep mentally young. Don't worry about acting your age. Be yourself. Whenever you're unsure about something, allow your pendulum to guide you.

Eat the right amount of good, healthy, nutritious food. Whenever you have doubts about certain foods or drinks, test them to make sure that they're good for you. If you nurture yourself with good quality food, every cell in your body will benefit as a result, and your energy levels will increase. Remember, it's fine to break the rules sometimes. My pendulum tells me that ice cream isn't good for me, but I still enjoy eating it every now and again.

Keep physically active. Try a number of different forms of exercise and see which ones your pendulum recommends. Naturally, you should see your doctor before starting any form of vigorous exercise, but for gentler activities such as Pilates and walking, allow your pendulum to guide you. Your pendulum will also monitor your progress and levels of fitness.

Many people try to keep young by dyeing their hair, dressing youthfully, and using the language of younger people. However, none of these work unless they also maintain a youthful outlook on life.

You need to regain the hopes, ideals, dreams, and optimism you had when you were young. As people get older, they tend to take life more seriously and become set in their ways. They become less accepting of new ideas, and turn down opportunities to grow and learn.

I had an aunt who was always fun to be around. She was sociable, had plenty of interests, and thoroughly enjoyed life. However, when she reached the age of eighty, she decided she was old. There was nothing wrong with her physically. It was all in her mind. She lost interest in all the things she used to love, withdrew from the world, and in a matter of months turned into an old lady. She died a year or so later. I found it fascinating that someone as vibrant as her could change so dramatically in such a short period of time. As soon as she thought she was old, she became old. It was a lesson for me to do everything I can to keep mentally young for as long as possible.

A friend of mine is an emeritus professor of law. He's had a wonderful career, and even though he's now well into his eighties, he still goes to university every day. He told me that interacting with the students and enjoying their enthusiasm, exuberance, and laughter keeps him mentally young.

Your pendulum can help you keep young too. The mere fact that you own and use a pendulum shows that you're a freethinker who is curious about the world and wants to learn and grow.

At least once a week, swing your pendulum in a counterclockwise direction and release any negativity you may have unconsciously picked up during the week.

Every day, twirl your pendulum in a clockwise direction and send your love out to the world. Think of all the things that make you happy, and give thanks to the Universal Life Force for giving you the gift of life.

Your pendulum will help you assess how young you are. Start by asking it how youthful you are. You can do this by asking, "Is my attitude that of someone under the age of thirty?" Go up or down a decade, depending on the answer you receive. Once your pendulum has confirmed the decade, you can determine the exact age, if you wish.

Another experiment is to make a list of activities that you enjoy doing, but haven't done for a while. Ask your pendulum to indicate the activities that make you feel youthful. Once you've found out what they are, set aside enough time to start doing some of the activities that keep you young at heart.

Make a list of the people you interact with regularly, making sure you include both positive and negative people. Ask your pendulum which ones you have the most fun with and which ones drain you of energy. Try to spend more time with enthusiastic, positive people, and less time with people who make you feel tired and negative.

Lower your stress levels as much as possible (see resolving long-standing emotions and feelings on page 200 and controlling stress on page 212). Stress makes you feel and look older than you are. At least once a week—once a day, if possible—do something enjoyable for yourself. This might be spending time on your own reading a book. It could be meeting a friend for coffee, going to a social event, relaxing in a hot bath, attending a class, or going to a movie. Every so often, try something you haven't done before. All learning is good, and it could mean the start of a new hobby or interest. Your pendulum will be able to give you advice on all of these things.

Spend time with people younger than you. This should include children and grandchildren, if you have them. You might volunteer to help out at a school or recreation center.

The mother of a school friend of mine volunteered at a local school, helping children learn to read. She is now 102 years old and lives in a retirement community. One of her most regular visitors is a former student who she helped more than forty years ago. She is still reaping the rewards for the good deeds she did all those years ago.

Laugh often. Many people look as if they haven't had a good laugh in years. We all know that life can be a serious business, but we're still allowed to laugh. It costs nothing, and is good for your mental and physical health. Spend as much time as you can with people who make you laugh. You might enjoy visiting a comedy club or going to a humorous play. You can watch comedies and stand-up comedians on TV. Make a list of them, and ask your pendulum which ones you'd enjoy the most. Laugh out loud, even if you're on your own. As well as making you look younger, laughter releases endorphins and makes you feel good.

Be kind and forgive others. Life is too short to hang on to old hurts and grudges. You'll be happier and find every-day life much smoother if you refuse to hang on to emotional baggage. Your pendulum will help you release any negativity in your life (See eliminating fears, doubts, and worries on page 64 and resolving long-standing emotions and feelings on page 200).

Exercise regularly. All movement is good, and you'll feel better and younger as a result. You don't need to take up long-distance running or any other competitive sport. Make a list of the activities you think you'd enjoy, and ask your pendulum for advice on which one to choose.

Make plans. It's good to have something to look forward to. Decide what you want to do, then start preparing for it. You might decide to take an overseas vacation. Your pendulum will be happy to advise you on where to go. Study brochures, read books, and decide what you'd like to see and do on the vacation. Check the cost of airfares and accommodation. Once you have all the necessary information, you can start putting money aside for the vacation, and ultimately book and take the trip.

All of these things will help you maintain your youth, vitality, and zest for life. Your pendulum really can be your elixir of life.

18. Evaluating Every Area of Your Life

What do you want from life? Do you want to be rich? Do you want vibrant health? Would you like more friends? A happy home and family life? Happiness and peace of mind? Everyone's heard of people who made a lot of money but were total failures in their private lives. The happiest people are those who are successful in every area of their lives.

Strangely, many people seem to be unaware that they're neglecting whole sections of their lives. Someone might work eighteen hours a day, but justify it by thinking that the extra money will help their family. Meanwhile, their family is at home, wishing the person was with them, and possibly harboring feelings of resentment at his or her absence. If one area of life becomes the total focus for someone, other areas inevitably suffer.

You can use your pendulum to assess any area of your life you wish. For a general assessment, you could divide a semi-circle into quarters and label them physical, mental, social, and spiritual. Suspend your pendulum over each section in turn, and ask questions about how well you're doing in that aspect of your life. You might ask, "Am I as physically fit as I'd like to be?"; "Do I receive enough mental stimulation every day?"; "Am I happy with the amount of time I spend socializing?"; and "Am I developing spiritually?"

You might prefer to create a percentage chart and ask your pendulum to indicate how well you're doing in each area.

If you're unhappy with anything your pendulum tells you, you should ask it questions about what you need to do to rectify the situation. Act on what you learn. Nothing will happen unless you're prepared to make changes. This may not be easy, and you should do it one step at a time.

A neighbor of mine was unhappy with her level of fitness and decided to take up jogging. However, she was so exhausted after her first run that she never did it again. Her chances of success would have improved dramatically if she'd started with a short run and gradually increased the distance as her fitness improved.

Continue asking your pendulum questions at least once a week until your goal has been achieved. Once you've done that, continue doing this exercise every now and again to make sure you haven't slipped back into old habits.

Many years ago, after I'd given a talk on the pendulum, a man told me that he had to concentrate on his career, as he could see no other way of progressing in life. If he spent valuable time working on other areas of his life, he ran the risk of failure. I assured him that his work wouldn't suffer, and would in all likelihood improve if he paid attention to his home, family, and some form of recreation.

"All work and no play makes Jack a dull boy," he replied. He said it with a laugh, which made me wonder if he was dismissing what I'd said. Fortunately, he shook my hand

and said I'd given him a lot to think about. I hope he did what I suggested.

You can use a pendulum chart to see how you're doing in specific areas. Divide the chart into as many sections as necessary. You might, for instance, divide a chart into tenths to check on your finances, emotions, family, relationships, self-improvement, attitude, physical fitness, diet, generosity, and entertainment. You don't need to check on every area each time you do this exercise. Choose the ones that are most important to you at the moment and focus on them. After seeing improvements in these areas, start paying attention to one or more of the others and develop them further too.

19. Analyzing Character from Handwriting

Way back in the days when people communicated by mail, I regularly exchanged letters with a friend in the United Kingdom. Unfortunately, his mental health had been badly affected by experimenting with LSD when he was a student, and he was bedridden for about a week every month. He was a highly intelligent man who'd been a university lecturer until his illness prevented him from working. Most of the letters he sent me were informative and beautifully written. The ones he sent me while bedridden appeared to have been written by a different person altogether. During these times he thought he was Satan and was responsible for all the ills of the world. I didn't need to open the envelope to tell his condition when he wrote these letters, as his handwriting, normally clear and easy to read, became jagged and ugly when he was bedridden. The letters themselves were written in the same angry manner, with the slants going in every direction, clearly revealing his mental illness.

Although I couldn't see any evidence of his illness in his handwriting when he was feeling well, my pendulum picked it up immediately. I thought that I must be subconsciously influencing the pendulum, as his handwriting on these occasions was attractive, easy to read, and appeared normal in every way. I took several letters, including one from my friend, to a dowsing society meeting. I placed them in a row and asked people to tell me about the people who wrote the letters. They provided interesting insight into the character of the different writers, and all of them noticed something out of the ordinary about the writer of the letter I was most interested in. Most weren't able to tell me what it was that concerned them, but one member correctly said that my friend had a psychiatric illness and appeared to be two different people.

People don't write letters as much anymore, but it's still possible to find examples of handwriting, even if it's only the person's signature or a shopping list. In fact, with a pendulum, the example does not necessarily need to be handwritten, and could even be produced using block letters (printing). The process of analyzing a sample of handwriting with a pendulum is straightforward.

Look at the handwriting and see what feelings, if any, occur to you about the writer. Turn the sheet of paper over to determine how much pressure the person used when writing the message. This shows how much energy and intensity the person put into the letter. Turn the letter around and look at it sideways and upside down. This provides clues as to how neat and organized the writer is. Does the writing ascend or descend as it crosses the page? Writing tends to rise if the person is feeling positive and happy. Conversely, it descends if the person is feeling tired, pessimistic, or depressed. Does the writing slant forward, backward, or run straight up and down? Approximately seventy-five percent of people write with a forward slant, which shows they're leaning into the future. People who write with a backward slant tend to be introverted and look to the past.

Read the letter, preferably out loud, to see how the writing flows. Does it sound stilted or overly formal? Or does it sound as if the writer is speaking to you?

Suspend your pendulum over the bottom section of the sample. This is because the writer will be feeling more relaxed than he or she was at the start of the writing process. Ask your pendulum as many questions as you wish. If the writer is not known to you, you might start by asking: "Are the writer's intentions honorable?" If you receive a positive response to this, you might ask, "Should I reply to this letter?" You could make a list of what you might include in any reply, and hold your pendulum over each one to see which ones, if any, you should include. You can also ask the letter questions about the person's health and wellbeing, though you probably wouldn't do this unless you knew the person who'd written the letter.

If you're concerned about the writer of the letter, you can ask questions about what is going on in the person's life, if he or she is happy, and so on. If the content of the letter appears positive but you have a feeling that the situation might not be as glowing as the person wrote, you can ask questions relating to the person's mental and emotional states.

If you have doubts that the person who signed the letter actually wrote it, you can ask questions about the authorship. This may not necessarily mean anything. It's common for people in authority to ask other people to write letters for them, which they then sign. A few years ago, the secretary of a club I belong to received a letter from a member who couldn't read or write. The secretary gave it to me to look at, and my pendulum told me what we already knew. It was obvious that someone else must have written the letter for him. However, I wanted to make sure that the content of the letter contained his true thoughts and views, rather than those of the person who wrote the letter for him. My pendulum told me that that was the case. As a final check, the secretary read the letter to the member before the meeting to confirm this, and as it was, the letter was tabled.

In his book *The Practical Pendulum*, Bruce Copen describes a method of handwriting analysis that he was taught by an Italian friend who had worked for Mussolini during his rise to power. In the course of his work, he received a large number of anonymous letters. He tested all of them with a pendulum, and on the occasions when the letter writers were arrested for writing threatening letters, his handwriting analysis was correct ninety percent of the time.

Place the letter on a table in front of you and hold your pendulum over it. If it swings toward and away from you, the person has an exceptionally good character. If the pendulum swings from side to side, the person has good character. However, if the pendulum's movement changes to an ellipsis, the person has a disorganized mind. Counterclockwise gyrations indicate someone who lacks integrity, while clockwise gyrations indicate a negative character (Copen 1974, 39).

I've experimented with this and found it reasonably accurate. The big disadvantage with this, though, is that it provides very little detail.

The pendulum is a useful tool for people who've studied graphology. A graphologist friend of mine uses his pendulum whenever he notices variations in a letter writer's T crosses and the placement of the dot above a lowercase I. The T cross and dot placement are especially interesting, as the writer has to interrupt the flow of his or her writing to add the cross and place the dot in position. This freedom enables the writer to create the cross in whatever manner appeals to him or her. Usually, the T cross and dot placement will be much the same throughout the letter, and they're easy to interpret. Variations in the T cross and dot placement cause problems in interpretation. Fortunately, a pendulum can answer questions about any graphological variations such as these.

My friend holds his pendulum over an example of the most frequently used T or dot, and observes the pendulum's movements. He then holds it over a variation and again notes the pendulum's response. Usually, the pendulum will respond differently over the variation, and he can ask the pendulum questions about it to help his analysis of the handwriting.

20. The Pendulum and Abundance

The word *abundance* means different things to different people. Most relate it to financial wealth, but it can also be considered a synonym of success. The word changes its meaning according to circumstances too. A multi-millionaire's definition of abundance is likely to be very different than that of someone who's unemployed or living on minimum wage. When it comes down to it, everyone wants just a little bit more than they already have. My definition of abundance means having a plentiful supply of all the things I need in life. Most of these have nothing to do with money. For me, and I suspect many others, love, friends, good health, joy, kindness, and happiness are worth much more than dollars in the bank.

Your pendulum can help you decide what abundance means to you. What would you like more of in your life? Once you've decided on that, your pendulum will help you determine if you're willing to do whatever is necessary to achieve it. In some cases, the price might be too high. You might want to become a billionaire, but if you're not prepared to set goals, constantly focus on them, and work hard, chances are you'll never achieve them. That means they're really just dreams, not intents or goals.

Let's assume you'd like more friends. Here is a process.

Ask your pendulum if it would be beneficial for you to have more friends. I'm sure you'll receive a positive response to this, as the richness of your life is largely determined by the quality of your relationships. If you're genuinely seeking abundance, good friendships are vital.

Assuming the answer is positive, the next step is to decide where to go to meet people who may become friends. Make a list of places you could visit, or clubs you could join. Ask your pendulum questions about each of them, and find out which one it recommends.

Go online and learn as much as you can about the club or place. Spend some time thinking about friendships you enjoyed in the past, starting from early childhood. Think about all the people you've enjoyed spending time with during your life, and tell yourself that you're a lovable person who gets on well with others.

Give your pendulum a clockwise spin and remind yourself of all the happy moments in your life. Tell yourself that you're warm, friendly, approachable, and loving. You deserve to have more friends. To help the process, remind yourself that to have a friend you need to be a friend, and you are going to be a good friend. As the pendulum slows down, thank the universe for attracting the right people to you. Repeat this step every day until you've made some friends.

Be kind, gentle, and friendly with everyone you meet. Show interest in them and their lives. Do what you can to help them in some way. Be natural, spontaneous, considerate, and genuine. Accept other people as they are. Reveal something about yourself too. If you do all of these things, people will accept you as you are and you'll gradually make good friends.

Use the same process for any other area of life you'd like abundance in.

In addition to this, every morning when you wake up, say a sincere thank you to the Universal Life Force for all the wealth and prosperity you currently have. Express your gratitude for all the blessings you enjoy in your life right now, and name as many of them as you can. You might like to write a list of all the blessings you already have and then see if you can add something new to it every day.

If possible, perform this morning ritual with your pendulum. Spin it counterclockwise and ask the Universal Life Force to eliminate any negativity that may be present in your life. Ask it to repel any energy that could be negative to you. Be as specific as possible. If, for instance, you're having problems with a colleague at work, ask for the difficulties to be diffused and dissolved.

Once the pendulum has stopped moving, spin it clockwise and ask the Universal Life Force to attract happiness, contentment, health, and prosperity to you. Naturally, you can add anything else you wish to attract, such as kindness, gratitude, friendship, opportunity, and peace of mind.

As the pendulum slows down, visualize yourself in the near future exactly as you want to be. Finish by saying "Thank you. Thank you. Thank you."

Whenever you have a spare moment during the day, visualize yourself as the prosperous person you're going to be. Then start becoming that person.

21. How to Raise Energy

Have you ever felt exhausted after a day at work, and all you wanted to do was blob out in front of the TV or go to bed? Have you also had the experience of being in this situation but then had a friend contact you suggesting you go out and do something exciting? The chances are all the feelings of tiredness miraculously disappeared and you suddenly had all the energy you could ever need.

Life is more enjoyable when you have an abundance of energy and can make the most of everything that comes your way. Of course, there'll be times when you don't want a great deal of energy. You might, for instance, want some quiet time to sort matters out in your mind, or to simply rest and relax.

Fortunately, your pendulum can help you raise your energy whenever you need it. You can spin your pendulum in a clockwise direction and ask it to raise your energy to its highest level (or any other level you desire). Thank the pendulum for doing this as it slows down and stops.

You can also ask your pendulum to tell you what your energy level is. You can do this using a chart or by placing the pendulum inside a glass. If you're using a chart, the pendulum will swing to indicate your current level. If you're using a glass, start by asking if your energy level is more than fifty percent. The pendulum will probably hit the side of the glass to indicate yes. If it does this, ask if it's more than sixty percent. Continue doing this until the pendulum fails to tap the side of the glass. If you wish, you can continue by asking about one percent increases until you get your answer. Of course, if the pendulum fails to respond at fifty percent, you'll have to go backward and ask about forty percent, thirty percent, and so on until you get an answer.

Once you know your current level, you can ask the pendulum to raise it to whatever level you wish. Do this by simply asking it if it will help you raise your energy to whatever level you desire. If you get a positive response, you can spin the pendulum clockwise and thank your pendulum for raising your energy.

Apart from health problems, the most common reasons for lack of energy are stress, overwork, grief, and relationship difficulties. Obviously, these need to be resolved to enable you to progress in your life. Once whatever has caused the loss of energy has been dealt with, your energy levels should return to normal.

If you regularly suffer from a lack of energy, you should ask your pendulum questions about why this is the case and what you can do to remedy the situation. You should also see your doctor.

You can also use your pendulum to send energy to someone else. If someone tells you that they're feeling exhausted, you can offer to send them energy. This is a six-step process.

1. Ask the person who needs more energy to sit down, take a few deep breaths, and relax.

2. Sit down with your pendulum and swing it clockwise. Ask it to raise your energy to its highest level. As it slows down and comes to a stop, thank it for doing this.

3. Ask your pendulum to tune in to the other person's mind. It will give you a positive response once it has done this.

4. Swing your pendulum clockwise again and ask your pendulum to send fifty percent of your available energy to the person who needs it. Watch the pendulum as it circles, and explain why you are doing this. As it slows down, thank your pendulum for its help.

5. Stand up and shake your arms and legs for several seconds. Sit down again and spin your pendulum clockwise. Ask it to raise your energy to its highest level. Again, thank it for enabling you to send energy to someone who needed it, and for restoring your energy to its highest level.

6. Wait until the pendulum has stopped moving before getting up. Ask the person to stand up, and ask how he or she is feeling. Often, you won't even need to ask as the change in the person's energy levels will be obvious.

You can also do this exercise if the person is not with you. Once they've given you permission to raise their energy, you can spin the pendulum over a photograph of them (see dowsing photographs on page 219) or write the person's name on a piece of paper and dowse over that.

22: The Pendulum and Your Chakras

Dictionaries define the aura as an electromagnetic energy field that surrounds all living things. As it's part of every cell in the body, it's more correct to describe it as an *extension* of the body, rather than something that surrounds it. The aura reveals a great deal about the person's character, emotional state, mentality, health, vitality, and path through life. The aura expands and retracts in size depending on the person's vitality and health. It contains all the colors of the spectrum, and these change depending on the person's moods and emotions. This is where expressions such as "in the pink," "green with envy," "feeling blue," and "red with rage" come from.

Chakra is a Sanskrit word that means "wheel." Chakras are revolving, wheel-like circles of subtle energy located inside the aura. They are powerful batteries that energize the entire body. Their task is to absorb the higher energies, including the Universal Life Force, and transform them into a form that the physical body can utilize.

The seven main chakras are situated alongside the spinal column and energize the physical and subtle bodies they're associated with. The state of each chakra reflects the health of the organs it is related to, and can be open, closed, blocked, and in or out of balance. Any changes made to the chakras to restore them to balance have an immediate effect on the physical body. It's rare for anyone to have all of their major chakras open and in balance at once. Most chakra difficulties are caused by fear, worry, and stress.

Root Chakra

The root chakra is situated at the base of the spine in the area of the coccyx. It keeps us grounded to the earth and provides feelings of security and self-assurance. It provides energy, vitality, strength, and persistence. It is concerned with self-preservation and controls our fight or flight responses. The root chakra also looks after our sense of smell, and the solid parts of our body, such as bones, teeth, and nails.

When the root chakra is understimulated, the person will feel timid, nervous, and insecure. When it's overstimulated, the person will be self-centered, domineering, and obsessed with power, money, and sex.

Sacral Chakra

The sacral chakra is situated in the lower abdomen about two inches below the navel, at the level of the sacrum. This chakra is concerned with the fluidic functions of the body and the sense of taste. It represents creativity, emotional balance, sexuality, optimism, and the ability to get on well with others.

When the sacral chakra is understimulated, the person is likely to experience arthritis, urinary problems, or sexual dysfunction, as well as feelings of powerlessness. When this chakra is overstimulated, the person will be manipulative, aggressive, and self-indulgent.

Solar Plexus Chakra

As its name suggests, the solar plexus chakra is situated between the navel and the sternum. It is concerned with confidence, self-esteem, happiness, and personal power. It relates to the absorption and assimilation of food, good digestion, and feelings of physical well-being. It is also associated with the eyes, as everything looks better when the person feels happy and contented.

When the solar plexus chakra is understimulated, the person will be overly sensitive, lack confidence, and feel powerless. When it's overstimulated, the person will be an overly demanding, obsessive, perfectionist and workaholic.

Heart Chakra

The heart chakra is situated in the center of the chest, in line with the heart. It relates to both personal and uncon-ditional love, friendship, harmony, healing, and the sense of touch. It enhances compassion, self-acceptance, and respect for self and others

When the heart chakra is understimulated, the person will be overly sensitive, overly sympathetic, fearful, and feel sorry for him or herself. This person is likely to be codependent. If this chakra is overstimulated, the person will be possessive, controlling, moody, and difficult to get on with.

Throat Chakra

The throat chakra is situated in the neck at the level of the throat. It is the chakra of self-expression and communication, especially that which is spoken. It enhances idealism, love, understanding, peace of mind, kindness, the truth, and faith in oneself.

When the throat chakra is understimulated, the person will be weak, timid, devious, unreliable, and uncommunicative. When this chakra is overstimulated, the person will be arrogant, overbearing, inflexible, and sarcastic. He or she will speak at great length, but have no interest in listening to others.

Brow Chakra

The brow chakra is situated in the forehead, just above the eyebrows. This chakra governs the mind and controls all the other chakras. It's often called the "third eye," as it's concerned with psychic and spiritual matters. It makes us aware of our spiritual natures and helps us pick up other people's thoughts, feelings, and intuitions.

When the brow chakra is understimulated, the person will be hesitant, non-assertive, diffident, and likely to suffer from tension headaches. When this chakra is overstimulated, the person will be proud, authoritative, unbending, and devious.

Crown Chakra

The crown chakra is situated at the top of the head. Artists show it as a halo around the head of someone who is spiritually evolved. The crown chakra stabilizes and harmonizes the conflicting sides of our natures. It controls the mystical and spiritual side of our beings that give us insight and understanding into the interconnectedness of all living things. It brings enlightenment and a sense of being at one with the entire universe. It can be activated only after the other chakras have been mastered and are in a state of balance.

When the crown chakra is understimulated, the person will be withdrawn, inhibited, reticent, and feel unable to participate in any of the joys of life. When this chakra is overstimulated, the person will be frustrated, depressed, angry, and critical. He or she is likely to suffer from cluster or migraine headaches.

Chakra Balancing

This is a nine-step process.

1. Ask the person whose chakras you are going to balance to lie down on their back. Suspend your pendulum over the person's root chakra and ask, "Is (person's name) root chakra in good health?" If the pendulum gives a positive response, nothing further needs to be done to this chakra. It's a sign that work needs to be done on this chakra if the pendulum gives a negative response. Make a mental note of this and move on to the sacral chakra.

2. Check all the chakras in the same way, asking if each chakra is in good health.

3. The next step is to determine which chakra is the most negative. Do this by holding the pendulum over each of the chakras that gave a negative response and asking, "Is the (name of chakra) the most negative?" Ask additional questions to establish the order of the negative chakras.

4. Fill a glass with water and place the fingers of the hand that does not hold the pendulum into it. Hold the pendulum over the chakra that is most negative and swing it in a counterclockwise direction to remove the negative energies. Visualize the negativity coming up the pendulum, into your arm, across

your shoulders, down your other arm, and into the glass of water. Thank your pendulum, silently or out loud, for releasing the negativity from the chakra. Explain what you're doing to the person whose chakras you are balancing. Continue to give thanks until the pendulum comes to a stop.

5. When the pendulum comes to a stop, take your fingers out of the water and wash both of your hands thoroughly under running water. Empty the glass of water and wash it thoroughly before filling it up again. Do not reuse the water you've tossed out for any other purpose.

6. Repeat this process with all of the negative chakras until they have all been treated.

7. Repeat step one with all of the chakras to make sure that all the negativity has been removed and the chakras are in balance. Sometimes you'll find that some of the negativity still remains, and you'll have to perform step four again over any chakras that are still hanging on to some negativity. The chakras are not in balance until you receive a positive response from all seven.

8. Swing your pendulum clockwise and visualize the color green as you pass the pendulum over every part of the person's body. Green is a healing color,

and it's important to send this color to all of the chakras, and to the rest of the person's body as part of the process. Thank your pendulum for balancing the person's chakras as it slows down and stops.

9. Tell the person whose chakras you've balanced to relax for a minute or two before getting up.

After the chakra balancing, the person should feel revitalized and ready for anything. Some people will tell you they never felt better. A pleasant side effect is that you'll also feel revitalized after performing a chakra balancing.

Naturally, you can't balance your own chakras in quite the same way. However, you can ask questions about each chakra and repair them using a glass of water and a counterclockwise swing of your pendulum. In practice, it's better to find someone who can perform the process on you, and you can repay this person by balancing his or her chakras in return.

The chakra balancing process opens up the hearts and minds of the people you work with, and you'll find many of them will be happy to discuss the causes of the negativity after a session. Emotional factors are responsible for causing blockages in the chakras. If someone seems open and receptive, I'll discuss these while I'm checking each of the chakras in step one. Usually, though, I'll wait until I've finished before gently explaining the most likely causes of the blockages. These are:

- Root chakra: lack of confidence, self-doubt, unable to let go of the past

- Sacral chakra: self-centeredness, selfishness, difficulty communicating with others

- Solar plexus chakra: low self-esteem, feelings of despair and hopelessness

- Heart chakra: difficulty handling emotions, lack of empathy

- Throat chakra: frustration, problems expressing inner-most feelings

- Brow chakra: inability to accept the world as it is, living in a fantasy world in preference to reality

- Crown chakra: stubbornness, rigidity, inability to connect with others

You can balance people's chakras even when they're not with you. The simplest way is to hold your pendulum and ask if any of the person's chakras are out of balance. Obviously, there's no need to do anything if you receive a negative response. If the response is positive, ask that any imbalances be corrected. Your pendulum will circle until the chakras are fully restored and balanced.

This method is quick and easy, but provides no information about where the problem occurred. You can gain a clearer picture by obtaining a chakra chart and dowsing each chakra individually. Start by making the intent that the chart represents the person's body and then proceed with the chakra balancing as if he or she was present.

If you don't have a chakra chart, you can draw one on a sheet of paper, or simply visualize the chakras as you go through the chakra balancing process.

23: Working with Your Guides and Angels

Angels are spiritual beings who attend to God. They also serve as God's messengers and are go-betweens for God and humanity. There are an infinite number of angels that can be called upon for help whenever necessary. In addition to this, everyone has their own guardian angel whose job is to protect, guide, and provide companionship to the person they are responsible for.

Spirit guides are people who have passed over into the next life. Although they've reached a high spiritual level where they are, they retain an interest in what is occurring in this world. They are willing to provide guidance and help when it's asked for.

You can use any type of pendulum to communicate with your guardian angel or spirit guide. Angels, in particular, respond well to crystals, and I know many people who have a crystal pendulum that they use only when communicating with the angelic realms. I have several crystal pendulums in my collection, and my favorite one is selenite. Selenite is a translucent white crystal that seems to glow with a special radiance when polished. It is frequently used for protection, but it also helps people think and grow spiritually. Celestite is also a popular crystal for angelic pendulums. It comes in a variety of colors, ranging from white to brown. It helps people hear messages from the angels clairaudiently, which means the messages appear as thoughts inside their heads. Rutilated quartz, sometimes known as "angel hair" is popular too. This isn't surprising, as the inclusions of fine rutile look like strands of hair that have been trapped inside the crystal. Quartz amplifies angelic communication, making it easier to send and receive angelic messages.

The pendulum is one of the most effective ways to communicate with your guardian angel or spirit guide. All you need do is sit down quietly with your pendulum and tell it that you would like to communicate with your guardian angel, a specific angel, or your spirit guide.

Make a list of everything you wish to discuss with your angel or spirit guide. You might like to create a special atmosphere by using a white candle. Your normal pendulum will work well, but at some stage you'll probably obtain a crystal pendulum that you'll use only when communicating with the spiritual realms.

Ask if your angel or guide is prepared to talk to you. Usually, you'll receive a yes response. On rare occasions, the answer will be negative. Your angel might be busy with some other task, or you may be upset, angry, or stressed. You can ask your angel for help whenever necessary, but ideally you should be feeling calm and relaxed when communicating with your angel. Accept a negative response when it occurs, and try again later.

Once you've made contact, ask your angel or spirit guide everything you want to know. When you first do this, you might like to ask your guardian angel for his or her name. To do this, you'll need to go through the alphabet one letter at a time, asking your angel if each letter is the first letter of the name. Repeat this as many times as necessary to find out your guardian angel's name.

Thank your spirit guide or guardian angel for spending time with you and answering your questions. Express your love and gratitude; smile as you say goodbye.

Spin your pendulum clockwise and send love to the whole world.

You can use your guardian angel, or any other angel, whenever you do any dowsing. All you need to do is start by asking, "Do I have the angels' blessing for the questions I'm going to ask?"

A positive response will let you know that the angels are present and are willing to help you. If you receive a negative response, you should ask further questions to find out why they aren't willing to bless your session with the pendulum. You may find that the angels feel you can solve the problem without their help. This occurs most often with people who call on the angels for advice about everything that's going on in their lives.

Guardian Angel Cards

Your guardian angel has your best interests at heart and will do everything possible to help you progress in this incarnation.

One good way to do this, which also strengthens your bond with your guardian angel, is to create your own set of guardian angel cards. All you need is a packet of file cards and your pendulum.

Write down the qualities you would like to develop on separate file cards. You can write down single words, phrases, or complete sentences to sum up the qualities you want to develop. Here are some possibilities:

- Express love

- Confidence

- Patience

- Self-expression

- Tolerance

- Compassion

- More enthusiasm

- Abundance

- Joy

- Grow in knowledge and wisdom

- Listen

- Integrity

- Strength

- Gratitude

- Think before speaking

- Trust intuition

- Develop spiritually

- Focus on my goals

- Exercise regularly

- Let go of the past

These are simply examples. Use as many of them as you wish, and write as many additional ones as you need. You can always add an extra card or two at any time.

The simplest way to use the cards is to mix them thoroughly and spread them out face up on a table. Ask your guardian angel to select the quality you should work on today, then hold your pendulum over each one in turn. Some people prefer to do this with the cards face down. This prevents them from inadvertently influencing the choice by overruling the movements of the pendulum.

Another method is to mix the cards and place them face down in a pile. Suspend your pendulum inside a drinking glass, and ask your guardian angel to reveal a number. The pendulum will tap against the side of the glass a number of times to indicate the number. When it stops, count down to that number card in your pile, and work on that particular quality.

I find it helpful to carry the selected card with me. Whenever I happen to see it during the day, it reminds me of my goal. Before going to bed, hold your pendulum over the card and ask your guardian angel questions about how you progressed with the particular quality. You can also ask if you should work with the card for another day. Continue working with the quality until your guardian angel tells you to choose another card.

24. Increasing Your Telepathic Ability

Telepathy is the ability of two people to communicate with each other without using the usual five senses. A common example of this is when a mother knows that something is wrong with one of her children, even though they might be thousands of miles apart. Telepathy often occurs spontaneously, such as when one person is in a moment of crisis and needs to contact a particular person urgently. An example of this is when someone contacts a friend or relative to say goodbye at the very moment of his or her death.

You have probably experienced many examples of mind-to-mind communication in your own life, and possibly didn't realize what it was. Here are two examples. Have you ever had a sudden urge to contact someone you haven't seen in years? The chances are this person was thinking of you and you picked up on the thought. Have you ever known who was calling you before you answered the phone?

You can use your pendulum to contact someone, even if the person is not carrying a cell phone and you don't know where they are. Sit down with your pendulum and think about the person you want to contact. Ask him or her to contact you urgently. Continue thinking along these lines until your pendulum produces a strong positive response. This tells you that contact has been made. Again, ask the person to contact you right away, and then relax. If you've been successful, you'll soon hear from the person you've been trying to communicate with.

You can make the visualization easier if you have a photograph of the person you're trying to contact. If you don't have a photograph, you might like to hold a piece of paper with the person's name written on it. These can help, but they're not essential.

Repeat this exercise as frequently as you wish until contact has been made. It's possible that the person received your message but was unable to contact you right away. Many years ago, I tried to contact a friend, not knowing that she'd just started acting in a play. She picked up my message, but was not able to contact me until the play was over. Remain confident that the person will contact you as soon as they can.

Your pendulum can help you develop your telepathic ability. Take out five cards from a deck of playing cards. Start with an ace, two, three, four, and five, all of the same suit. Ask a friend to mix these cards, and to take out one of them. He or she concentrates on this card while you gaze at your pendulum and ask, "Is it the ace?" then "Is it the two?" and so on. The pendulum will give a negative response to four of the questions, and a positive response to one. This should be the number that your friend was telepathically sending to you.

With practice, you'll be successful most of the time. Once you reach that state, you can alter the experiment slightly. Instead of asking questions of your pendulum, you can place it inside a drinking glass and ask it to tell you what number your friend is concentrating on. The pendulum will tap the side of the glass a number of times to indicate the number.

An interesting way to develop your telepathic ability is to send thoughts of love to someone you're close to. Sit down somewhere you're unlikely to be disturbed. Hold your pendulum and think of the person you wish to send love to. You might think of the last time you were in each other's company, or a pleasant activity you enjoyed together. It doesn't matter what you recall about the person, as long as they're happy memories.

Tell your pendulum that you want to send love to the person, and wait for it to give your positive response. Once your pendulum has agreed, think of how much you love the person and what they mean to you. Allow these feelings to build up in your heart. When your heart feels totally full of love, swing your pendulum clockwise and ask it to send all your love to the person you've been thinking about.

As the pendulum spins, visualize the person receiving your love. Thank your pendulum for enabling you to send love to this person. As it gets close to stopping, say "thank you, thank you, thank you."

The person will receive your love, but may or may not realize what has occurred. Sometimes, someone will tell you that they were thinking about you at the exact time you sent them love. You might receive a longer than usual hug or kiss the next time you meet. You may receive no response at all, but you will find that your relationship will deepen as a result of this.

You don't need to limit this experiment to people you love. You can send love to friends, acquaintances, and even total strangers. You can even resolve longstanding problems by sending love to people you dislike or don't get on with.

25. Divining with Your Pendulum

Divination has been practiced throughout human civilization, and is just as popular today as it ever was. Divination is the art of predicting future events or discovering hidden knowledge using a variety of techniques, such as astrology, palmistry, rune stones, and the pendulum. Divination is not the same as fortune-telling. Fortune-telling is the art of telling people about their future. Divination is the art of looking at a given situation from a different point of view. The word *divination* comes from two Latin words: *divinare* meaning "inspired by a god" and *divinus* meaning "the divine." This shows that divination was originally concerned with determining the will of the gods. Consequently, the information that came from the divination was advice and instruction from the gods.

You can use your pendulum on its own to ask questions about the future. You can also use it to help you gain additional information when you're performing any type of divination.

A friend of mine does aura readings on Skype. She claims that her accuracy has increased since she started using a pendulum. She does her readings exactly as she always has, but now holds her pendulum while doing them. She doesn't ask it questions, but pays attention whenever it responds to anything she or her client says.

A good friend of mine makes his living as a palm reader. Occasionally, he'll be puzzled by something he sees on a client's palm. He holds his pendulum over the hand, or the palm print he's made of the hand, and silently asks his pendulum questions to clarify what he's looking at. He's convinced that the quality of his readings has improved since he started doing this.

An astrologer I know prepares detailed written reports for his clients. He always proofreads them with a pendulum in one hand. His pendulum reacts when it needs to query anything he has written. This enables him to double check the information the pendulum has indicated and make any alterations or changes that he feels are necessary. As many people don't know what time of day they were born, he also uses his pendulum to help determine this.

Some years ago, I met a pet psychic who receives information from the pets he's reading for through his pendulum.

If you practice any form of divination, you'll find the additional insights that your pendulum can provide extremely useful. Start by asking your pendulum questions to clarify information provided by your normal tools. You'll find it an interesting experience, and one that may help you discover useful information for your clients that you wouldn't have learned otherwise.

Pendulum Numerology

Numerology is the art of interpreting the hidden symbolism of numbers. It is one of the oldest of the divinatory arts and has been practiced for at least ten thousand years. It's so old, in fact, that twenty-six hundred years ago, Pythagoras "modernized" it. Numerology reveals a person's character and future trends using numbers derived from the person's name and date of birth.

You can use basic numerology and your pendulum to predict the outcome of a future event. All you need is your pendulum, nine blank cards, and nine opaque envelopes. Write the number "one" on the first card and place it inside one of the envelopes. Continue doing this with all of the numbers up to nine.

Think of a question. It can be anything, major or minor. It can be relatively unimportant, such as the possibility of rain tomorrow, or something major, such as global warming or the possibility of peace in the world.

Mix the envelopes thoroughly while thinking of your question. It's important that you have no idea what number is inside any of the envelopes. Lay the envelopes in a row in front of you. Continue thinking of the question and your desire for an answer, while holding your pendulum over each of the envelopes in turn. Your pendulum will react differently over one of the envelopes. This is likely to be your positive response. The pendulum will give little or no response over the other envelopes. Open the envelope that your pendulum indicated. The number inside will answer your question.

Here are the readings for each number:

1. This is a time for new starts. You'll have plenty of enthusiasm and energy. Set worthwhile goals and aim high, as everything is going your way.

2. You'll need to be patient. This is not a time to push or force your will on others. Think, make plans, and wait for the right opportunity to move forward.

3. This is a good time for social activities, hobbies, and fun times with friends. Do whatever work is required, but allow enough time for relaxation too.

4. This is a sign of slow, steady progress. You may feel restricted and limited in what you can do, but any hard work you do now will pay off.

5. This is an excellent time to change anything. Think before acting, then make the changes you want.

6. Home and family activities are the focus at the moment. You may spend more time doing things for others than for yourself. There can be great satisfaction in this. Enjoy the pleasures of giving.

7. This is a time to think, learn, and grow inwardly. It's not a good time for material progress, but continue

with your plans, so you'll be ready to move ahead when the time is right.

8. This is a time of hard work, but any effort you put in now will pay off financially. Make sure to take time off every now and again for relaxation and social activities.

9. This is the perfect time to let go of anything that has outlived its use. This is likely to be difficult, but is important as far as your future is concerned. This is a good time to make plans for whatever it is you want to do next.

Sometimes the answer will be obvious, but there will be times when you'll have to think about how the answer relates to your question. Let's assume you were thinking about having a vacation in Hawaii. Number one suggests you start packing right away. Two means you'll have the vacation, but probably not as soon as you'd like. Three is a positive number and shows you'll have a wonderful time in Hawaii. Four shows that you have a number of tasks to get out of the way first; however, you'll get the vacation as your reward. Five is a sign of change, which could well mean a change of scenery. Six shows that something at home needs to be attended to before you start planning the vacation. Seven is a sign of patience—collect the travel brochures, start making plans, and book the trip when the time is right.

Eight is a sign that you'll be busy, but this will be financially rewarding. Set aside time for a special vacation. Nine is a sign that you need to let go of something connected with the past before taking the vacation.

If you wish, you can ask your pendulum further questions about the vacation by holding it over the card you chose.

Once you start experimenting with a pendulum, you're likely to be asked questions about it by friends who might be skeptical or think you're fooling yourself. Show them how to use a pendulum and let them have a turn. The skeptical ones may deliberately not allow the pendulum to move, and even the people who are not totally convinced might have trouble getting your pendulum to work.

Tell these people to think of a question. Hold the pendulum yourself, take a few seconds to relax and to tune into the person, and then ask the person to mentally ask the question. Your pendulum will respond, providing the same answer that they would have received if they'd asked it themselves.

This is also a good way of dealing with questions when you don't want to become personally involved.

26. The Pendulum and Tarot

The pendulum works well with the tarot and can be used in many ways to enhance your readings. You can use the pendulum to confirm what you're reading in the cards. A negative response, showing that the pendulum disagrees with what you're saying, can be just as useful, as it will force you to look more deeply into the cards by asking further questions.

Your pendulum can help you choose a card for any day. Thoroughly mix the cards and spread them out face down on a table. Ask your pendulum to find the card that will be most useful to you today (or tomorrow, or a particular date in the future). Move your pendulum slowly over the cards until it gives a positive response. Remove this card, but don't look at it yet. Continue passing the pendulum over the rest of the cards, just in case it responds positively over more than one card. If you end up with two or three cards, put the rest of the deck aside and place the selected cards in a row in front of you. Ask, "Which of these cards will be the most helpful card for me today (or future date)?" The card selected by your pendulum will have something to tell you about the day you indicated.

When doing a reading for yourself or others, you can ask the pendulum to choose the cards for you. Mix the cards, spread them face down on a table, and ask your pendulum to indicate the cards that you'll use in the reading.

Once the cards have been selected, you can place them in order using the first card selected in the first position, the next one in the second, and so on. Alternatively, you might ask your pendulum which of the chosen cards should be placed in the first position, then repeat this to place the other cards in the spread.

The pendulum can help you create the most helpful question to ask the cards. If you have just one question, ask the pendulum if this is the best possible question that can be asked at this time. Proceed with the reading if the answer is positive. If it isn't, you'll need to question your pendulum further until you have one that will prove most helpful to the other person.

If you have several questions, your pendulum will tell you which one would be the most useful to your client at this time.

While performing the reading, you can hold your pendulum over any cards in the spread and ask it as many questions as you wish to help clarify the situation. You can also use the pendulum to call on your angel or guide if you need additional help during the reading.

If you're like me and have a large collection of tarot decks, you can ask your pendulum which one to use. I have a deck that was made for me many years ago by a good friend. It's one of my most valuable possessions, and until recently I used it only when reading for members of my family. Several months ago, my pendulum suggested that

I use it when reading for a client. Since then, I've used it regularly. I enjoy telling clients about the talented friend who made it, and find it hard to understand why I'd limited it in the past to only family members who needed a reading.

27. Contacting Your Higher Self

Your higher self is your spiritual self, your conscience, your soul. It's the real, inner, unlimited you. It connects the mental and physical sides of your nature with the spiritual, and is the part that lives on and reincarnates when this lifetime comes to an end. It is calm and serene, and is unaffected by the actions of your mind, body, or ego. It is the real you, beyond your personality. Your higher self can provide guidance and wisdom to help you at every stage of your life. You make direct contact with your higher self whenever you're totally absorbed in doing something you love. You can communicate with your higher self more efficiently by developing your psychic abilities and trusting your intuition, which is your higher self talking to you.

Your pendulum will help you communicate with your higher self whenever you wish.

Sit down quietly with your pendulum in your hand. If it's moving, stop it. Take several slow, deep breaths to help you relax as much as you can.

Visualize your higher self. You might imagine him or her as a close friend sitting beside you. You might imagine yourself surrounded by a warm, loving, comfortable energy. You might imagine yourself sitting in the most beautiful place you can imagine, and have a sense that your higher self is there with you. It makes no difference how you visualize your higher self, as long as you have a sense of him or her before you start your conversation.

Silently or out loud say, "I have some questions and need to speak with my higher self." Pause and see what response your pendulum makes. If it gives a positive response, you can immediately start asking questions of your higher self. You might ask your higher self for a message that will help you handle matters going on in your life. You might ask for serenity and peace of mind.

If the pendulum fails to move, or gives a negative response, put it down. Stand up and shake your arms and legs vigorously. Drink some water. If you're feeling hungry, eat a few nuts or raisins.

Sit down again and think of your reason for calling on your higher self. As your higher self is an intrinsic part of you, you should be able to speak to and with it whenever you wish. Consequently, your higher self would never produce a negative response for no reason. If the problem is something that you can resolve easily, you may not need to discuss it with your higher self. If that's the case, swing your pendulum clockwise and thank your higher self for looking after you.

If your reason for communicating with your higher self is important, wait about thirty minutes before repeating the first steps. This time you should receive a positive response.

The ability to connect and communicate with your higher self will improve every aspect of your life. You'll view yourself, the people you deal with, and even life itself, in a completely different way. You might decide to have regular conversations with your higher self. This has many benefits. It will, for instance, enhance your intuition, empower you to set and achieve your goals, quiet your mind, and allow you to learn from all the wisdom that's freely available to you.

28. Interpreting Your Dreams

Everybody dreams, even people who claim they don't. Often, dreams are related to what the person did during the day before falling asleep. These dreams are usually unimportant and the person forgets them within seconds of waking up. Other dreams are more important, especially if they reoccur. These come from the dreamer's subconscious mind and provide insight into the person and their life.

Dreams speak to us in symbols, which is how the subconscious mind expresses itself. Sometimes the symbols are obvious, but usually they need to be interpreted.

Obviously, you can't interpret your dreams if you can't remember them. The first step to achieving this is to tell yourself that you will remember your dreams. Repeat this to yourself several times a day, and again before you go to sleep. I say this to myself firmly, putting the emphasis on a different word each time I say it. "*I* will remember my dreams tonight. I *will* remember my dreams tonight." I prefer to say this out loud, but you can do it silently if you wish.

Keep pen and paper, or some other form of recording device, beside your bed. This enables you to record your memories as soon as you wake up. Do this before you get out of bed.

Often, when you wake up you'll have a partial memory of your dream. Remain as still as you can, in the position you were in when you woke, and think about the dream.

Frequently, this allows more details to come into your mind. Record everything you can remember about the dream. It doesn't matter if it's not complete. Sometimes more information will come to you during the day, and you can add this to your memory of the dream. Writing your dream down and thinking about it later ensures that you'll remember dreams that would otherwise have been quickly forgotten.

The next step is to interpret your dream. Run through the dream in your mind and think of the main events that occurred in it. Take note of anything that could be related to what you were doing during the day before you had the dream. Recall any emotions you felt during the dream. Finally, think of any symbols that appeared in the dream.

Universal symbols are called archetypes. For instance, a red rose symbolizes love, a lion symbolizes strength, and an owl symbolizes wisdom. Unfortunately, many symbols are not as easy to interpret, and the meaning can alter depending on the dream. An anchor, for instance, might symbolize security, but it could also be a sign that the person is stuck or weighed down.

This is where your pendulum comes into play. You can use it to look at the theme, emotions, and symbols that occurred in the dream. I use it mainly to provide further information about the symbols. Dream dictionaries and books on the meanings of symbols are helpful, but they're often too general to provide the information you need to interpret your dreams.

I also find a pendulum helps my recall if I go through the dream while holding it in my hand. Any responses it makes encourage me to ask more questions. In addition, at the end of the story I'm able to ask it if the dream continues. If the answer is positive, I can ask questions that sometimes encourage more memories to come back into my mind.

29. The Pendulum and Your Past Lives

People have believed in reincarnation for thousands of years. Although most people have little or no recall of their past lives, knowledge of them can help people understand why they act and behave in certain ways in this incarnation. It can also help explain the reasons behind difficulties they're experiencing in this lifetime, and make them aware of any karma that needs to be repaid. It can provide valuable information about a person's purpose in this lifetime too.

There are many ways to explore past lives. These include crystal ball gazing, lucid dreaming, angelic communication, dowsing, and hypnotic regression. Hypnotic regressions are probably the most well-known of these. During a regression, various experiences that occurred in a previous lifetime are uncovered and explored. They're almost always helpful in helping the person understand why he or she acts certain ways in this lifetime. However, although the memories may be vivid, the experience is often lacking in details that can be checked later. This isn't surprising when you realize that throughout history, most people were illiterate, and many never traveled more than ten miles away from their homes. It wasn't unusual for people long ago not to know the name of the country they lived in.

Fortunately, a pendulum can provide this missing information. It may not be as exciting as a past life regression, but it can provide a great deal of useful information that would be difficult to learn using any of the other methods.

The process is simple, and you can do it for both yourself and others.

Start by asking the person what they want to learn from the experience. Some people want to know about karmic factors, others may have a fascination with a certain subject in this lifetime and want to know if it was something they did in previous lifetimes. Others want to resolve patterns of behavior, find out if someone is a soul mate, or simply appease their curiosity. Once you know what they're looking for, you can ask your pendulum the questions that answer the specific needs of your friend.

The first step is to ask the person's higher self for permission to explore one of his or her past lives. Hold your pendulum in your hand, and say, "I am with (person's name) and wish to speak to his/her higher mind. Do I have permission to connect with his/her higher mind?" As the person has already agreed that you can do this, your pendulum is likely to answer with a yes. You can then ask, "Do I have permission to explore (person's name) past lives?" Wait until you get an answer. Then say thank you.

The next step is to go back to a specific past life. You might ask for the person's most recent incarnation, a past life in a certain time frame, a past life in which the person had the same partner as they do now, or maybe a past life that created karma that is affecting the person's current life. Ask, "Can I connect with (the required past lifetime)?"

Assuming the answer is positive, you can now start asking questions about this particular life. I usually start by determining the person's gender. If the person is a woman in this lifetime, I'll ask if she was female in the previous life. If it's a man, I'll ask if he was male in the previous life. As we all experience lives as males and females, you can't assume that someone who is a woman in this lifetime was female in the lifetime you're exploring.

The next step is to determine the time period. I normally start by asking if it was in the twentieth century, and if necessary, go back a century at a time until the pendulum gives a positive response. Once you know this, ask if he/she was born in the first half of the century. If you get a no response, you'll know the person was born in the second half of the century, but it pays to ask this question all the same. You can now ask about the different decades, followed by individual years. If you wish, you can determine the month and day in the same way. I only do this when I feel that amount of detail will be helpful. You can speed up this process by using a pendulum chart with the months marked on it to determine the month, and a chart containing all numbers from one to thirty-one to determine the day. Once you have the date of birth, you can determine the date of death in the same way.

After this, you can ask questions about where the person was born. If the person has a feeling that he or she lived in a certain place, I'll ask about that first. This saves time if it happens to be correct. If I get a no response, I'll use one of two methods to learn where it was. You can name different continents and ask if the person was born there. Once you know the continent, you can ask about the different countries on that continent until you get the location. Alternatively, you can ask, "Does the name of the country where (person's name) was born begin with an A?" Go through the alphabet one letter at a time until you receive a positive response. Once you have the first letter, you can ask questions about all the countries with a name beginning with that letter. If you wish, you can ask questions about the location inside the country to determine the birthplace. A friend of mine has a historic atlas showing all the countries of the world at different time periods. Once he knows when the person was born, he opens the atlas to the correct page for that time period and map dowses it (see map dowsing with your pendulum on page 215) to determine the exact location.

You can learn the person's name in the lifetime you're exploring by going through the alphabet and divining it one letter at a time.

Follow the same process to determine the person's occupation or main activity. I usually start by asking about several occupations, such as agriculture, teaching, and medicine, in the hope that this will save time. If the person has an important creative interest, I'll ask about that too, as it's possible he or she made a living from it in the past life.

You might ask if people who are important to the person in this lifetime were with him or her in the past life. I inquire about parents, partners, children, and close relatives and friends.

You can follow this by asking about the person's marital status, children (if any), state of health, degree of affluence, and happiness in this lifetime.

You might continue with questions about the person's character, purpose in the lifetime you're exploring, degree of motivation, and anything else you wish to inquire about.

Finish by thanking the person's higher mind for allowing you to help the person by learning about this lifetime. Once you've explored a past life once, you can return to it as many times as you wish to ask more questions.

30. Pendulum Psychometry

Psychometry, sometimes known as psychic touch, is the art of gaining intuitive feelings and impressions about an object by touching or handling it. People who practice it are able to pick up information about people, places, and events by handling an object that has a connection with the person or place. Interestingly, some psychometrists pick up information about the object's past history, others describe the characteristics of the object's owners, and some almost become the object.

There's a famous story about Professor William Denton (1823–1883), a professor of geology. He was extremely interested in psychometry, and on one occasion tested his wife and his mother using tiny items that were wrapped in paper to prevent them from knowing what was inside. Professor Denton's wife was experienced at psychometry. When she was handed a packet containing carboniferous material, she immediately described swamps and palm trees. The professor handed her another packet containing lava rock from a volcanic eruption. She sensed a "boiling ocean" of golden lava. Professor Denton's mother didn't believe in psychometry. However, when she picked up a packet containing a fragment of meteorite, she immediately said: "I seem to be traveling away, away through nothing—I see what looks like stars and mist" (Buckland, 331).

Some people are extremely gifted at psychometry, and a few of these consider it a curse rather than a blessing. Frau Lotte Plaat, a Dutch psychometrist who sometimes worked for the German police, complained that she couldn't go into the British Museum as all "the objects were literally shouting their history" (Fodor 1974, 318). With practice, most people can learn to pick up information using psychometry, but unfortunately they're usually brief impressions that fade away almost as quickly as they appear.

Fortunately, your pendulum can take these momentary flashes of information and provide answers to questions about them. It's not unusual for psychometrists to practice other forms of divination as well as psychometry, and of these, the pendulum is arguably the most useful method. Geraldine Cummins, a British medium, is an example of this. In her work, she combined psychometry with automatic writing.

The only way to become good at psychometry is to practice it as often as you can. Personal objects, such as rings, watches, and jewelry, are the best to start with. Avoid coins, as you'll get too many conflicting messages from all the people who have handled them before they arrived in the hands of their present owner.

Hold or handle the object to gain impressions. Some people find it helpful to close their eyes while doing this, and others appear to go into a trance. However, most people remain in their normal state and receive impressions through their hands and fingertips. Pause and wait for any impressions or sensations to appear. If nothing comes after thirty or forty seconds, think about the object and ask yourself who is most likely to have handled this object often. See if you can pick up something about this person. Where was it made? Where did it come from? Hopefully, thoughts and ideas will come into your mind. Continue holding or touching the object until the impressions fade. If you're holding the object, place it on a table or some other stable surface.

Pick up your pendulum and swing it in a clockwise circle. Tell it that you're psychometrizing whatever it happens to be, and that you need it to help you clarify some of the information you've received. Thank it for helping you do this. Pause until the pendulum stops moving.

Hold the pendulum over the object you're psychometrizing and ask it questions relating to the information you've received. Continue doing this until all your questions have been answered.

Put the pendulum down and pick up or touch the object you're psychometrizing. Take slow, deep breaths and wait to see if any further information comes to you. Allow about a minute to see if the information you've gained from the pendulum will encourage further impressions to come into your mind.

As soon as possible, write down all the information you learned during the pendulum psychometry session. It's helpful to keep a record of your progress, and if you psychometrize the item again later, you can compare the two readings.

31. Psychic Protection

I've met many people who laugh at the idea of "psychic protection." These same people live in a house that protects them from the elements. They invest their money to earn interest, but also to keep it safe. They buy insurance to protect them from a variety of possible calamities.

Psychic protection is at least as important as these, as we all experience our share of stress, pressure, resentment, and hostility as we go through life. We also need psychic protection when we're feeling drained mentally, emotionally, or physically.

At one time I worked for a married couple who argued with each other all day, every day. Almost every evening I returned home with a headache, as the environment at work was so stressful. It's easy to pick up negativity from others. The news we see on television or hear on the radio is seldom good, and is another source of negativity. Our own negative thoughts and feelings undermine us and can be considered a form of self-inflicted psychic attack.

Although some people scoff at the thought of psychic protection, many people make use of it without knowing it. Do you have a lucky charm, such as a horseshoe, four-leaf clover, or a "lucky" rabbit's foot? When you travel, do you carry a St. Christopher medal with you? These are all forms of psychic protection. Astronaut Edward White took a St. Christopher medal, a Star of David, and a gold cross with him when he went to the moon (Paine 2004, 11). If that had been me, I'd have done exactly the same.

Fortunately, your pendulum can help you protect yourself and your loved ones from intentional and unintentional psychic attacks.

Unintentional psychic attacks are easily dealt with. All you need do is swing your pendulum counterclockwise and ask that all the negativity be removed from your mind, body, and spirit. When the pendulum stops, swing it clockwise and fill yourself with strength and positive energy.

Deliberate psychic attacks are a different matter, especially if you have no idea who is targeting you. Many victims of this experience what is known as "hag syndrome." The victim wakes up with the sensation of a crushing weight on his or her chest, and an inability to move. Sometimes they see shapes, hear strange sounds, or smell unpleasant odors.

Other common signs of a psychic attack are nervous exhaustion created by feelings of dread, fear, and hopelessness, and an unexpected loss of weight. Loss of appetite, nausea, nightmares, poltergeist phenomena, and unexplained bruising can also be indicators of psychic attack.

Naturally, you'll be emotionally involved if you suspect that you're being psychically attacked. Because of this, it's better to ask someone with no emotional involvement in the matter to ask questions for you. Make a list of questions, then go for a walk, sit in a park, or enjoy watching the water in a fountain, river, lake, or sea while your friend asks the questions for you. Water is very beneficial if you feel you're being attacked. Accept the answers your friend's pendulum gives you, even if they're not what you'd hoped to hear.

The next step is to prevent the person from ever attacking you again. It makes no difference if you know who the person is or if you have no idea who it could be. In addition to your pendulum, you'll need a length of cord between one and three yards long. Make a mark at one end of the cord to identify it, as you'll need to untie the knots at the end of the exercise in the same order they were tied in at the start.

In this step you're going to tie nine knots in the cord. This symbolically binds the person to prevent him or her from attacking you again. While you're tying the knots, think about the person who is attacking you and tell yourself that you've had enough of his or her evil thoughts and deeds. Think of the outcome you desire as you tighten the knots. Start by tying a knot at each end of the cord, then a third knot in the center. The fourth knot is tied halfway between the knot at the left end of the cord and the center knot. The fifth knot is tied halfway between the knot at the right end and the one in the center. The sixth knot is tied halfway between the knot at the left end of the cord and the next knot. The seventh knot is tied halfway between the knot at the right end of the cord and the next knot. The eighth knot is tied halfway between the center knot and the knot to its left. The ninth knot is tied halfway between the center knot and the closest knot to its right.

Take the cord outside and bury it in earth for three days. This makes the person who has been attacking you powerless, as you have bound him or her securely with the nine knots. Burying it for three days demonstrates your feelings about this person's thoughts and deeds. Make a note of the time of day that you do this.

After burying the cord, spin your pendulum counterclockwise and release all the negative energy from every part of your mind, body, and spirit. Follow this by spinning it clockwise to fill yourself with positive energy. Do this at least twice a day for at least three days.

After three days, dig up the cord at the same time of day that you buried it. Untie the knots in the same order that you tied them in. As each knot comes free, say out loud, "(Person's name, if you know it), you have lost your power over me." You might even spit after saying these words, to emphasize your contempt of the person. Increase the energy with which you say these words each time, so that you're shouting by the time you've undone the last knot.

You now need to destroy the cord, as the power of the curse, which is what a psychic attack effectively is, has been transferred into it. Set fire to the cord, and while it's burning, say good riddance to the person who's been attacking you.

Immediately after burning the cord, spin your pendulum counterclockwise to release any residual negativity that might still be present. After this, spin the pendulum clockwise to fill yourself with strength, positivity, and feelings of well-being.

32. Communication with Plants

It wasn't until I spoke at a gardening club that I discovered how many gardeners use pendulums to help them look after their plants. One of them told me that when she moved house she'd asked her pendulum to indicate the best place in her property to set up a vegetable garden. She was very happy with the results. Another gardener told me how she'd never had any luck with rhododendrons until she asked her pendulum where she should plant them. Someone else told me that he uses his pendulum to test the quality of the soil.

All of this brought back memories of a neighbor I had many years ago who asked her potted plants every morning if they were happy. Usually she received a positive response. However, if the pendulum gave a negative response, she'd ask further questions, such as "Would you like more sun?" or "Do you need more water?" She'd act on the answers until her pendulum told her the plant was happy.

You can use your pendulum to choose plants at a garden center. Ask them if they'd be happy coming home with you, and tell them you'll do everything you can to ensure they're happy and will thrive in your garden. Sometimes, instead of using a pendulum, I choose my plants by body dowsing (see appendix).

Let's assume you've bought or been given a new plant. It may even be a packet of seeds. You're not sure where to plant it in your garden. Hold your pendulum over the plant or packet of seeds and start asking questions. Ask if the plant should be planted now. If not, ask further questions to determine the best day and time to plant it. You can ask the plant where in your property it would grow best. Once you've determined where to plant it, you can ask questions about the soil, and find out how much compost and fertilizer the plant needs. You can also ask questions about the drainage, amount of clay in the soil, and anything else you wish to know. You can even ask the plant what size hole needs to be dug for it to be planted in.

An alternative method is to walk around your lot with the plant in one hand and your pendulum in the other, while asking where would be the best place to plant it. Your pendulum will give a positive response when you're in the right place. When you're ready to plant it, you can use your pendulum to decide which way the plant wants to face. It can also tell you what compost and fertilizer it needs, and if it's happy with any nearby plants. You can also ask questions about underground water, radiation, and anything else that is relevant to the happiness and health of your new plant.

If you prefer, you can draw a diagram of your lot and determine the answers to these questions by holding your pendulum over different parts of your hand-drawn map.

Sooner or later, you're likely to experience a problem I had. My wife and I bought a rosebush for a specific position in our garden. However, when we got it home, my pendulum told us the best place to plant it was in the backyard where no one, except us, would see it. There were two possible solutions to this. We could plant it where the pendulum told us, especially as we knew it would do very well in that position. Or we could ask the pendulum if the plant would grow satisfactorily in the position we had originally chosen. In addition, we could ask the pendulum what we needed to do to the soil in that position to help the rosebush thrive. The pendulum gave us good advice on this, but in the end, we decided the bush would be happiest in the backyard. It was the right decision. The rosebush thrived, and whenever we see the people we sold the house to many years later, they tell us that the rosebush is still flourishing in our former back garden.

Companion gardening occurs when two or more plants harmonize well and produce better crops or flowers as a result. You can use your pendulum to determine the compatibility of any two plants in your garden. You can do this by asking the two plants individually if they'd be happy together. Alternatively, you could place the plants about two feet apart and suspend the pendulum between them. The plants will be happy if the pendulum swings two and fro between the two plants or moves in your positive direction. This can be extremely useful with potted plants, as you can easily place compatible plants together and ensure incompatible plants are kept well apart.

A number of studies have shown that plants respond well to the human voice, especially female voices. The

Royal Horticultural Society conducted a monthlong study involving ten people who read literary and scientific works to tomato plants. Each person was responsible for one tomato in a pot. The soil, amount of water, variety of plant, and levels of sunlight were identical in all of them. At the end of the month, the plants that had been talked to by a woman had grown an average of one inch taller than the plants spoken to by men. One plant, which was read to by Charles Dickens's great-great-granddaughter, grew about two inches taller than all the others (Alleyne 2009).

Given that plants respond well to the human voice, you can enhance this further by spinning your pendulum clockwise over your plant while talking to it. Thank it for choosing you to look after it. Encourage it to grow. Say anything you wish to your plant. Speak positively and vary your intonation.

Once the pendulum stops circling, ask your plant if it needs more sunlight, more nutrients (such as potassium or calcium),or anything else you can think of to ensure that it's happy.

You might also like to ask your plants if they enjoy music. If they do, find out what type of music they like and play it for them regularly.

If you have a sickly plant, you can hold your pendulum over it to confirm that it's unwell. Start mentally sending positive thoughts of health and well-being to it. Your pendulum will stop giving a negative response and will change to produce your positive response, showing that you've removed the negativity and also given the plant a dose of positivity. When doing this, I touch trees and larger plants with one hand while holding my pendulum with the other. With smaller plants, I hold my pendulum over them.

33. The Pendulum in Your Garden

Many years ago, we moved to a new house. On one side of the driveway was a row of macrocarpa trees (related to the pine family). They gave us privacy and made a fine display. Shortly after we moved in, the tree closest to the road died. We immediately planted another macrocarpa seedling in the same spot. Initially, it grew quickly, but about two years later it also died. This was puzzling, as all the trees had been thriving for at least fifteen years before we moved in. I used my pendulum to test the soil and found that the ground where my tree had died was acidic, while the soil the other trees were planted in was alkaline.

About the time we moved in, the people behind us subdivided their property and a new house was built on what had been their front yard. The property was down a long right-of-way, and all the cables and pipes for the services were buried in the ground less than two yards from our row of trees. I can only assume that something in the supply of these had caused the soil at the bottom of our property to become acidic.

Once I discovered this, we were able to resolve the problem, by adding limestone and organic compost to the soil to make it more alkaline. The tree that we planted on the spot is now as healthy and tall as the older trees. Until we moved, fifteen years later, I regularly checked the soil with my pendulum. I showed the person we sold the house to how to do it, and last time I drove past, the tree was still there and was looking just as healthy as the others.

It's a simple matter to check the soil on your property. Take a sample of soil, hold your pendulum over it, and ask if the soil is healthy. If it isn't, you can ask further questions to determine what it needs, and then rectify the problem. You can test the quality of fertilizers and supplements in the same way.

You can also test to find out if the soil is suitable for a particular plant. Place a small sample of the soil on a table, and place the seed or seedling a few inches away from it. Hold the pendulum between them. The soil will be suitable for the plant if the pendulum starts swinging to and fro between them.

If you're planning to use fertilizer, place a small sample of it on the table to create a triangle of soil, seedling, and fertilizer. Hold your pendulum between the soil and the fertilizer. You should receive the same to and fro response. Hold the pendulum between the seedling and the fertilizer and test that too. Finally, hold your pendulum over the center of the triangle. If all three elements are in harmony, the pendulum will spin clockwise.

Your pendulum can help you decide which plants would thrive best in your garden. This is particularly useful for people who have a vegetable garden. Before planting anything, you can make a list of a dozen or more vegetables you'd like to grow (See how to dowse from a list on page 227). Ask your pendulum questions about which of them would do best in your garden. You can also ask questions about the right time to plant the seeds, the right type of compost, the amount of water required, and anything else you can think of to ensure you have a good crop.

You might be fortunate enough to design and create your own garden on an empty site. This gives your pendulum plenty of scope, and you can ask it questions about the type of garden you'd like to have, which plants to buy, and where to plant them. You might want to include other factors, such as a pétanque court, an ornamental arch, a gazebo, a sculpture, or some other feature.

Derek, a friend of mine, bought his home partly because it was on a large, flat lot and he'd always wanted his own labyrinth. This is a maze-like, usually circular, path that people walk to find spiritual meaning and peace of mind. Many years before, he'd walked the famous labyrinth at Chartres Cathedral in France. He wasn't a gardener and had no desire to do anything else. However, once he'd completed the labyrinth, he decided it needed to be surrounded with vegetation of some sort to make it look more attractive and to give him privacy when he walked it. He consulted his pendulum numerous times, and over a period of five years he developed an amazing garden based on the four elements of fire, earth, air, and water.

One quadrant is dedicated to fire and, following his pendulum's advice, he created it around a sundial. During summer, the plants in this area bloom with magnificent red, orange, and golden hues. The earth quadrant is created around a cairn of river rocks. He placed a fountain in the center of the water quadrant and has a wind chime sculpture as the focal point of the air quadrant.

During the process of designing and creating his garden, Derek fell in love with gardening, and today his entire property is one huge garden.

You might decide on a theme for your garden. Years ago, I saw a prosperity garden in a home in Dorset, England. It was a long, narrow, formal garden with a central path leading to a gazebo at the far end. Several semi-precious objects had been buried in the garden to attract prosperity to the people who lived in the house. The owner of the house used a pendulum at every stage of the project, and still uses it for advice on the care and well-being of the plants in the garden. "It wouldn't be good for prosperity if all the plants died!" he told me.

If I had the chance to create my own garden, I'd start by asking my pendulum about different themes. Depending on the nature of the land available, I'd be keen to have a knot garden, a fragrance garden, or maybe even a Zen garden. Once I had a theme, I'd make a rough sketch and ask my pendulum what it thought about it. Using the pendulum's responses to my questions, I'd gradually create a plan that I could work with. Once the basic layout had been done,

I'd ask my pendulum for advice on soil, fertilizer, irrigation, plants, and everything else that occurred to me during the process. It would be a huge amount of work, but it would be extremely rewarding.

34. Communication with Your Pet

Your pendulum provides an excellent way to interact and communicate with your pets and other animals. You can check your pet's emotional health and understand the reasons why he or she behaves in a particular way. You can diagnose any health problems that may occur, and will be able to enjoy pleasant conversations that will give you insights you'd never learn using any other method. Doing this will also enable you to see situations from the animal's point of view. As a result, the bond between you and your pet will strengthen.

Another benefit of communicating with your pet in this way is that your intuitive skills will expand and develop. With practice, you may discover that you can communicate with your pet telepathically, and will not necessarily need your pendulum as a communication aid.

Hugging a loved pet is one of the best feelings in the world. Spending time with a pet can restore your spirits in an instant, because they're endlessly supportive, forgiving, empathetic, and loving. Their healing energy can even increase the length of their human companions' lives. A study of patients with heart disease found that pet owners were more likely to be alive one year later than the patients who didn't have a pet (Friedmann, Katcher, Thomas, Lynch, and Messent 1980, 307-312). Interestingly, it made no difference if the person was rich or poor, married or single, surrounded by friends or a loner. Having a pet to love was the strongest single factor.

Most pet owners believe they can communicate with their pets. This communication can improve enormously with the help of your pendulum. It's a five-step process.

1. Spend several minutes cuddling, talking to, and playing with your pet. Keep talking, but gradually reduce the play to gentle stroking and patting.

2. Stop making physical contact, but continue talking for a minute or two. When you stop the stroking, your pet is likely to look at you inquiringly, but will sit or lie down beside you. This might happen again when you stop talking. If it does, give your pet one or two gentle strokes and then stop.

3. Produce your pendulum and mentally tell your pet that you love them. Ask your pet if they can "hear" you. A positive response shows that they did, and you can move on to the next step. If you get a negative response, swing your pendulum clockwise and, while it's spinning, mentally tell your pet how much you love them. Think of happy times you've spent together and how you're hoping your pendulum will help you and your pet become even closer. When the pendulum stops, say "thank you" three times.

4. Pause for several seconds and then ask your pet if they can hear you. Don't worry if you get another

negative response. What you're doing is something new, and your pet might not understand what you're trying to do. Spin the pendulum clockwise again and thank your pet for enriching your life in so many ways. Continue sending thoughts of love until the pendulum stops. Just before it stops, say "I love you."

5. Follow this by thinking "thank you" three times. Wait for about sixty seconds, as your pet might still send a positive response to your pendulum. If it does, you can start asking it questions. If it doesn't, try the experiment again a day or two later. Continue doing this until your pet gives a positive response.

Once your pet has given a positive response, you can ask any questions you like. You might be surprised with some of the answers you receive. Don't take anything personally. Pets can lie, or it's possible you're asking questions that they can't be bothered answering. It's a sign that your pet has had enough if he or she stops responding to your questions. Mentally tell them "I love you. We'll talk again soon."

Unfortunately, though, animals can't tell us what is wrong when they're ill. This is when your pendulum comes into its own, as you can ask it any questions you might have about the state of your pet's health.

The first step is to hold the pendulum over your pet and ask if the problem is a major one. If it is, you should take it to a veterinarian as quickly as you can.

If the problem doesn't appear to be particularly serious, you can ask your pendulum what you can do to help your pet. You can ask about the best food or supplements, and anything else you feel might help. Often, with pets, sleep is the best remedy.

Recently, my daughter's dog started vomiting after every meal. She seemed perfectly well apart from this, and my daughter's pendulum assured her that it wasn't serious. She asked more questions and learned that her dog had found cough lozenges at a neighbor's home and eaten them. She was concerned about her dog's stomach, but the pendulum assured her that it was fine. Two days later, her dog was fit and well again.

You can test your pet at any time to see if they are in good health. If your pendulum tells you that something is wrong, you can do something about it immediately, rather than wait until your pet is in severe pain.

Your pendulum will also help you determine the best foods for your pet. Your pet might, for instance, like two commercial brands of pet food. Your pendulum will be able to tell you which one is better for your pet.

The packaging on one product may be beautiful, but that doesn't necessarily mean the contents are of good quality, and your pet might have a good reason for refusing to eat it. You can use your pendulum to find a good quality food that your pet will enjoy.

You can also test any supplements before giving them to your pet. Ask questions about the benefits your pet should receive as a result of taking it. You should also ask if there are any potential negative outcomes.

Like humans, animals need exercise. Your pendulum will tell you if your pet is getting enough exercise. You may think you're giving them sufficient exercise, but especially if they're a large animal, you mightn't be giving them enough. Conversely, if your pet is getting on in years, you might be giving them too much.

Abbé Mermet regularly located missing animals using his pendulum and a map. On one occasion, a farmer asked him to locate a missing cow. The farmer was concerned, as he was looking after the cow for an elderly widow. After the farmer drew a map of the area, the Abbé suspended his pendulum over it and told the farmer that the cow had fallen into a precipice one hundred meters deep, and was lying at the bottom, dead, with all four feet in the air. The farmer was puzzled, as he wasn't aware of the precipice. However, when he went to the site, everything the Abbé had told him was correct, even the cow lying with all four feet in the air (Mermet 1959, 207-208).

It's not necessary for an animal to be lost for the pendulum to locate it. Monsieur Joseph Treyve, manager of a horticultural center in Moulins, France, and a keen dowser, always used a pendulum to locate wild boar before he went hunting (Fairley and Welfare 1982, 181).

35. Eliminating Negativity

Have you ever walked into a room and immediately sensed negativity? The first time I can recall experiencing this was in my first job in publishing. When I walked into my boss's office, he and his secretary were sitting on opposite sides of his desk. This was normal, and they both turned and smiled at me, which was also normal. Yet there was an unpleasant atmosphere in the room, which made the conversation awkward. I learned later that they had had an argument, and the negativity was still present in the room even though they both tried to act as if nothing had happened.

Negative energy can be created by arguments, stress, illness, violence, and death. This pervasive energy can linger indefinitely, creating an unpleasant environment for everyone who has to use the space.

Fortunately, your pendulum can help you eliminate all forms of negative energy.

The first step is to ensure that you've protected yourself. Protection is always important, but is even more so when dealing with any form of negativity (see psychic protection on page 155). Stand with your legs slightly apart and your arms by your sides. Close your eyes, take three slow, deep breaths, and then visualize a pure white light coming from the Universal Life Force and entering your body through the top of your head. Visualize it filling every cell of your body, and then overflowing and surrounding you in a bubble of pure white protective light.

Stand in the center of the area where you feel negative energy and ask your pendulum, "Are there any negative energies here?" This may sound like an obvious question, as you, and probably others, will have sensed the negativity. However, you should ask it, just in case the negative vibes you feel are caused by something else. A friend of mine once did an energy clearing that didn't work. She discovered that the negativity she sensed was caused by some spilt milk that hadn't been cleaned up properly and had soured. You will ask this question again, once you've cleared the area, and this time the answer should be no.

Leave the area and cleanse yourself by closing your eyes and visualizing a pure white light entering your body and filling it to overflowing with healing, cleansing, protective energy. Once your body is full of this light, visualize it expanding to fill the room you're in, and continuing to grow until the entire building is full of white light. Take several deep breaths of white light and open your eyes. Ask your pendulum if you have enough power and energy to remove the negativity that is causing the problem. Your pendulum should give a positive response. If it doesn't, repeat this step again.

Return to the room with the negative energy. Stand in the center of this room and swing your pendulum counterclockwise. Say, "I ask the Universal Mind to remove all negativity from this room. Please dissipate any negativity, no matter what the cause or where it came from, and ensure it loses all power to harm or hurt anyone ever again. I need this room to be filled with love and light again. I allow my pendulum to continue making counterclockwise circles until all the negativity has gone. Thank you. Thank you. Thank you." Continue expressing thoughts along these lines until your pendulum stops moving.

This step replaces the negativity with positive energy. Swing the pendulum clockwise and say, "I ask the Universal Mind to fill this room (space) with peace, light, and divine love. Please allow this positive energy to spread out to every part of this room, fostering joy and laughter, light and love, happiness and positivity everywhere it goes. I allow my pendulum to continue making clockwise circles until this room is filled with positive energy again. Thank you. Thank you. Thank you." Continue thinking positive thoughts until the pendulum stops moving.

The final step is to repeat the question you asked in step one: "Are there any negative energies here?" The answer should now be no. Ask this question again a day or two later, and again one week later. If you receive a positive answer to this question, repeat the process, but this time start and finish by walking around the room in a counterclockwise direction holding a lighted sage smudge stick. These can be obtained online and at New Age stores. Be careful when using them, as they produce a great deal of heat. Keep a container of water nearby and hold a dish under the stick as you walk counterclockwise around the room. After you've walked around the room at the end of the process, move the smudge stick around your body to cleanse any negativity from your aura.

You don't need to wait until you're aware of negative energy before asking, "Are there any negative energies here?" You should check your home and workplace on a regular basis to make sure that you're living in the best possible environment.

You can use this same process to get rid of negative entities and ghosts.

36. Tracking Cables and Water Pipes

It's expensive to hire someone to locate buried pipes and cables. People who are searching for water, oil, minerals, or anything else often call on the services of a dowser, as they need to make sure they're drilling in the right place.

You're more likely to be searching for cables or water pipes that lead to your home. The easiest way to do this is to think about the pipe or cable you're divining for while holding your pendulum and walking along the sidewalk in front of your property. Place a peg in the ground at the position your pendulum indicates. Move closer to your house, and repeat the process. Do this two or three times, placing a peg in the ground each time your pendulum reacts. By doing this, you'll gradually mark out the course of your power cables, water pipes, or anything else you're seeking.

When dowsing larger areas, place the first peg in the ground where your pendulum told you, and then walk thirty feet away. Walk in a circle around the peg, and your pendulum will react twice to indicate the course of whatever it is you are searching for.

About twenty years ago, the pipe bringing water to the house we were living in at the time burst. As the water main was underneath a long concrete driveway, we were facing a horrendous bill if the workmen had had to dig it all up to find where the pipe had burst. Fortunately, I was able to dowse the driveway and locate the exact position of the broken pipe. I told the plumbers where to dig, and the pipe was repaired for a fraction of the price we'd originally been quoted. This is just one example of the many times dowsing has saved me money.

Instead of walking over your property, you may find it more convenient to locate your water pipes and power cables by dowsing over a map of your property. Map dowsing is covered on page 215.

37. Dealing with Harmful Radiations

We are surrounded by radiations, both good and bad. The rays from the sun, for example, are essential for life on earth, but they're also harmful in excessive amounts.

You can see this for yourself by turning your television on and holding your pendulum an inch or two away from it. Your pendulum will probably give a negative response. Gradually move it away from the screen and see how far away you get before the pendulum stops moving. You might have to move as much as seven feet away. After checking your television, you can also find out how far the radiation extends on either side of your television. Once you've done this, you'll probably choose not to sit within the area your pendulum has indicated.

You can also test your computer screen, cell phone, microwave oven, and other electric or electronic devices. However, this radiation is not necessarily harmful.

Even though we're usually not consciously aware of them, the earth's radiations have a profound effect on us. Georges Lakhovsky demonstrated that the geological nature of soils played an important role in the incidence of cancers. He found that soils that absorbed external radiations, such as sand and gravel, were associated with the lowest incidences of cancers, while impermeable soils, such as clay and mineral ores, were associated with the highest (Lakhovsky 1939, 5-13). The terrain is only one factor in the causes of cancer, but most researchers accept that harmful earth radiations play an important role in a number of illnesses. These include arthritis, chronic fatigue, goiters, headaches, lumbago, rheumatism, sterility, and tuberculosis.

The most harmful radiations come from geopathic stress, which is energy created by the earth's electro-magnetic field. Problems arise when this energy is affected by underground running water. People living in houses located on geopathic stress lines will have weakened immune systems, and those sleeping on stress lines may, in time, develop serious health problems. Geopathic stress is a natural phenomenon, in the same way that poisonous plants and animals are. We should avoid or protect ourselves from anything that's poisonous, which is why we need to be aware of geopathic stress. You can't protect yourself if you don't know it's there.

You can use your pendulum to check your home for geopathic stress. This is especially important in the bedroom and any other room where people spend a great deal of time. You should change the position of any beds that are crossed by geopathic stress lines. Often, moving the bed a foot or two is all that's required.

It can be helpful to draw a plan of your house before starting to dowse it. Mark on this any lines of geopathic stress that your pendulum finds. You'll find that these lines will continue beyond the room into other areas of the house.

You'll also find that if your home has more than one level, these lines will show up in the same places on each level.

Start the dowsing process by protecting yourself. You should always do this, but it's particularly important in this case, as you're dowsing for noxious energy. Stand at the front door and tell your pendulum, "Show me any geopathic stress, underground water, or any other form of earth energy that is capable of affecting anyone who lives in this house."

Step inside and visit each room in turn. Walk from one side of the room to the other, and repeat this with the other two sides. This should pick up any lines of geopathic stress in the room. In addition to this, I walk from side to side through the entire room in a criss-cross fashion to make sure that all lines of geopathic stress are found.

Another way to check for geopathic stress involves removing all the electric and electronic devices from the room you're testing. Once you've done that, walk slowly in a straight line from one corner of the room to another with a compass in your hand. The arrow of the compass should remain constant, but it will react noticeably if you cross a geopathic stress line. Before acting on this, check that you're not walking over a power cable or a water pipe.

To eliminate these harmful radiations, Georges Lakhovsky invented the Lakhovsky Loop (also known as the Lakhovsky Coil). This consists of loops of wire that are tied around the frames of beds to eliminate harmful radiations.

His loop used an oscillating circuit that created resonance, and increased immunity and resistance to disease. Lakhovsky loops can be purchased online, but they're not hard to make. Instructions on how to make them can be found on the internet.

38. Dowsing Your Home

The word *home* should create happy thoughts in our minds. This is because our home is much more than a house or apartment. Our homes become part of us, as they're full of our personalities, interests, and memories. The bookshelves tell others what we like to read, and many books are kept because of the pleasure they gave us or because they were given to us by someone we love. The photographs and pictures on the walls remind us of the people we love, too. Ornaments and other decorations were all bought for a purpose and provide pleasure and happy memories. Our home is our special, secure, safe place where we can relax and be ourselves.

Consequently, just the thought of home should make us feel happy. Do you feel good when you return home from work? Do you look forward to getting home?

If you have any doubts or concerns about your home, your pendulum will help you rectify them. You can do this by moving from room to room with your pendulum, asking it anything you wish to know. Alternatively, you can dowse over a drawing or plan of your house (see map dowsing with your pendulum on page 215).

Start by standing outside your house, and asking your pendulum if there's any harmful energy running under or through your home. If the answer is yes, find out how many lines of energy there are, then locate them. You can do this by walking through your lot and house while asking your pendulum to indicate areas of negativity. Usually, lines of noxious energy follow underground streams of water. Sometimes, negativity can be caused by disagreements, stress, and violence. Both forms of negativity can be removed by your pendulum (see eliminating negativity on page 175 and dealing with harmful radiations on page 181).

Once you've removed the negativity, stand in the kitchen and ask if there are any problems or concerns in this room. The kitchen is often considered the heart of the home, and it's important that this room is free of any concerns. You'll already know if your kitchen is a happy place to work in, as you should feel content whenever you spend time in it. No matter how happy you feel in this room, check it with your pendulum. If it detects any concerns, find out what they are and resolve the problem. This will restore the harmony that should be in the kitchen, and will spread it throughout the house.

Repeat this in every room of the house, paying particular attention to the family rooms and bedrooms. Usually, any problems will be minor ones. Your pendulum might tell you to fix a broken window catch, replace a light bulb, or to let more light and fresh air into a room that's seldom used.

Once you've done this and each room has told you that everything that needed to be attended to has been resolved, stand in the center of the house and revolve your pendulum counterclockwise. Ask the Universal Life Force (or whatever power you choose) to remove any negativity that may be present in any part of your home and lot. Thank it for making your home a happy and joyful place to live. Continue doing this until the pendulum stops. Spin it in a clockwise direction and give thanks to the Universal Life Force for making your home a happy, loving, and secure place for everyone who lives in it. Continue giving thanks until the pendulum stops moving.

39. The Pendulum and Your Diet

Everyone knows that they should be supplying their physical bodies with enough good food and water to satisfy its needs. Everyone eats the wrong foods at times, but this is unlikely to be a problem as long as it is done occasionally, rather than as a regular part of the person's diet.

You can test any food or drink with your pendulum. You can find out if it's good or bad for you, if you're allergic to it, and even if you have too little or too much food on your plate. You can find out if it contains any preservatives. You can determine its freshness. If you're thinking of taking a supplement, you can ask your pendulum if you need it and if it will be beneficial for you. Your pendulum will even tell you the correct amount to take.

A friend of ours is allergic to monosodium glutamate, a commonly used flavor enhancer, and has been admitted to hospital several times after accidentally consuming it. She always carries a pendulum with her and tests everything before eating it. To avoid attracting undue attention in restaurants, she holds her pendulum under the table and points at the food with her free hand. I've shown her how to hand dowse (see appendix), but she prefers to use her pendulum, as it's never let her down.

During World War I, André Simonéton, a French engineer, almost died after contracting tuberculosis. He had five difficult operations, and while close to death, heard two army doctors whisper that he would soon be dead. However, he wasn't ready to die. As soon as he could, he started using a pendulum to choose food that was healthy and good for him. His health gradually returned, and he enjoyed a long and active life. He wrote a book on his health and nutrition discoveries that was published in 1949, he fathered two children in his late sixties, and was playing tennis well into his seventies (Nielsen and Polansky 1977, 99). He is the perfect role model for anyone wanting to improve their health through diet.

You can test food and drink in a variety of ways. In each case, start by asking your pendulum if the food is good for you: You might hold your pendulum over food you're thinking of eating and ask questions about it. You could hold a sample of the food in one hand and your pendulum in the other.

You might hold the pendulum over the back of your hand, then slowly move your hand until it's over the sample you're testing. It's a positive sign if the pendulum makes the same movement throughout this exercise.

You can place your hand between the pendulum and the food you're testing. A positive response is a sign that the food is good, and a negative response indicates the opposite.

You can even write the name of the food on a piece of paper and hold your pendulum over that. If the item or pen and paper are not available, you can simply think of the food and ask your pendulum about it. Suitable questions

to ask are, "Is this food good for me?"; "Is this food in harmony with my body?"; and "Is this food harmful to me?" It
can be interesting to ask these questions before and after
the food has been cooked.

If you're testing food for someone else, let the pendulum
gyrate over the food and then hold the pendulum over the
person's hand. If the pendulum continues to make the same
movement, the food will be suitable for this person to eat.

An interesting way to test different foods is to place a
wide selection of them on a table. Include foods that you
know are good for you, such as fresh fruit and vegetables,
but also include tinned foods, convenience foods, chocolate, candies, and sodas. Hold your pendulum over each one
in turn and ask if the food is good for you. Most of the
answers will be just as you'd expect. However, if you're doing
this experiment at a time when your blood sugar is low, you
may get a positive response when it's held over something
sweet. Don't allow your personal likes and dislikes to affect
these experiments. Remain impartial and let the pendulum
decide which foods are good, indifferent, or bad for you.

It can be helpful to make a list of all the foods and
drinks you and your family consume regularly, and hold
your pendulum over each one in turn. Ask if the particular food or drink is beneficial for you. Once you've done
that, ask the same question for other family members.
You're likely to find that some foods are good for certain
family members, but are either neutral or bad for others.

Once you've checked your list against every member of the household, you'll know which foods are beneficial for everyone living in the house.

You can test different foods with a pendulum when you're shopping. If, for instance, you're wanting butter and find a number of different brands in the supermarket, you can determine which one of these apparently identical products is best for you.

Many years ago, at a dowsing society meeting, each member was handed a potato and a list of questions. These included determining the acidity or alkalinity of the potato when it was raw, when it was peeled and cooked in water, when cooked unpeeled, baked in an oven, cooked in a microwave, or fried.

Further questions were designed to see what minerals and vitamins were in the potato. It was entertaining and educational to see the number of questions that could be asked about a humble potato. These and similar questions can be asked about any item you're thinking of eating.

You can increase the positive energy of a meal by saying a blessing over it before starting to eat. You can measure this increase in energy with your pendulum. You can also perform blessings over water or anything else you plan to eat or drink (see prayers and blessings in pendulum clearing on page 36).

It's been estimated that the human body contains seventy-three trillion cells, all of which need water to perform their function and maintain good health. Ask your pendulum how much good quality water you need every day to remain fully hydrated. For most people, this is about four pints (two liters). You may need more or less. To make sure that you consume your required amount of water every day, pour that amount of water into a jug and place it somewhere you'll see it regularly during the day. Each time you see it, you'll be reminded to drink some. Most people are slightly dehydrated, as they don't think of water when they're not thirsty. You'll be amazed at how much water you drink when you see it numerous times a day.

As well as doing this, you can test the quality of the water with your pendulum. You can also send positive thoughts and energy into it by holding your pendulum over the container and giving it a clockwise spin.

40. Testing Foods with Your Pendulum

You benefit enormously from eating high quality, healthy food. These benefits include abundant energy, good health, good digestion, strong bones, and a lower risk of heart problems, diabetes, and cancer. However, as everyone is different, even foods that should be considered beneficial may not necessarily be good for you.

Genetically engineered (GE) foods have had their DNA altered to create changes that couldn't occur naturally. These modifications are done for a number of reasons, such as increasing the nutrient value of the food, increasing the crop yield, or enabling it to have a longer shelf life, lack seeds, be more colorful or appealing to look at, or be resistant to viruses, herbicides, and certain pests.

The first commercially produced genetically engineered food appeared on the market in 1994, and since then the number of products that have been modified in this way has grown enormously. Today, ninety percent of the corn, soybeans, and cotton grown in the United States come from genetically modified seeds (USDA). The scientists and producers who test and market these products claim that there's no greater risk in eating GE foods than there is in conventional foods.

However, many people around the world are skeptical about these claims, saying that GE foods have not been available for long enough to know if there are any long-term health risks involved, or to determine if the environment is being adversely affected. There are also concerns about the testing and regulations involved.

In Europe, GM foods are labeled, but this is not the case in the United States. One way to avoid genetically modified foods is to shop at stores that sell organic food, and to purchase products that are labelled USDA certified organic. This isn't always possible, though, and if you're concerned about genetically modified food, you can test foods with your pendulum before eating them. You might, for instance, ask, "Has this food been genetically modified?"; "Is this food good for me?"; or "Will this food harm my body?"

You need to think about more than genetic modification when buying food. Even foods that you consider safe to eat may contain harmful additives, contaminants, and pesticides that can cause serious health problems, including cancer. Preservatives, emulsifiers, sweeteners, colorings, and flavorings found in most processed foods are harmful too. Your pendulum will be happy to answer any questions you have about anything you're planning to eat.

In the case of fruit and vegetables you may find that your pendulum gives a different response after you've hand-washed them. By doing this, you may have washed off any residual pesticide on the skin. Some foods, such as avocados, have a thick skin. If you dowse one and ask if it's good for you, you might receive a negative response. However, you may receive a completely different response if you cut it open and hold your pendulum over the flesh.

41. Healing with Your Pendulum

When people ask a friend of mine how he is, he replies, "I'm full of radiant vitality!" I love the sound of the word *vitality*. It means he's fit, well, and full of physical and mental energy. We all want to be full of radiant vitality.

If I'm feeling unwell, I ask my pendulum questions about what is wrong, what caused it, and what I need to do to restore my health. I'll also visit my doctor, if necessary, as I believe that the pendulum should be used in conjunction with conventional medicine, rather than on its own.

Let's say you have a headache. The chances are you know what caused it. You might have experienced an unusually stressful day at work. You might have been a victim of road rage, heard some distressing news, or had a disagreement with someone. You won't need your pendulum to tell you what was responsible for your tension headache. However, if you suddenly get a headache for no apparent reason, you should ask your pendulum questions about it.

You might ask if a rest or a good night's sleep will cure it. Should you take an aspirin? Would it be a good idea to make an appointment to see your doctor?

You can then ask what caused the headache. Was it stress? Eyestrain? Something you ate? Alcohol? Lack of sleep? Dehydration? There are many possible causes.

A friend of ours discovered she was allergic to chocolate when she asked her pendulum why she was experiencing so many headaches. When she avoids chocolate, she enjoys excellent health. She can go up to six months without eating it, or even thinking about it. Eventually, though, something minor will trigger her craving for it. She might see an advertisement for chocolate, for instance, or happen to see someone eating it. She fights the craving for as long as she can, but eventually she eats some, knowing that it will be followed by a bad headache. This headache is bad enough to send her to bed for a few days, but once she's recovered from that, she doesn't even think of chocolate again until, months later, the craving starts again.

It's not easy to diagnose or heal yourself using a pendulum, as you're intimately involved in the process. This means you're likely to unconsciously influence your pendulum with your own fears and worries and receive an inaccurate diagnosis. Because of this, I rarely ask my pendulum questions about any health problems I experience that seem concerning. However, on a few occasions, I've asked other people to ask the questions for me.

There are a number of methods that can be used to diagnose a problem. Father Jurien, a well-known French dowser in the early twentieth century, used to painstakingly ask questions about every organ in the body (Bulgatz 1992, 275), such as, "Is there a problem with the patient's gallbladder?"; "Is there a problem with the patient's stomach?"; and "Should the patient make an appointment with a specialist?"

An easier method is to ask the person to lie down on his or her back. Scan every part of the person's body with the pendulum, while watching carefully for any irregularities in its movements. Ask questions whenever this occurs. Obviously, you need to send the person to a doctor if you uncover anything that could need medical attention.

If the person isn't with you, you can draw a sketch of his or her body, write the person's name above it, and scan the sketch with your pendulum. Whenever possible, you should obtain the person's permission before doing this.

If the problem is minor, your pendulum will advise you on the best course of treatment. It might suggest homeopathy, naturopathy, Bach flowers, herbs, acupuncture, exercise, a change of diet, an aspirin, or conventional medicine.

If you have a potential remedy nearby, you can hold the pendulum over it and ask if it would help cure the ailment.

Many years ago, I was at a barbecue on a beach. One young man hit his thumb with a hammer while erecting a tarpaulin to provide shade. Another man, who I assumed was the young man's father, produced a pendulum and held it over the aching thumb. The pendulum swung counterclockwise for about sixty seconds, then stopped and swung clockwise. The young man declared that the pain had gone and finished erecting the tarpaulin.

I spoke to the man with the pendulum, and he told me it was a trick that builders did. When you hold the pendulum over the hurt area, the pendulum gives a negative response. This briefly increases the pain, but then it starts to diminish. The pendulum stops and then produces a positive movement to indicate that the pain has gone.

I've used this technique on myself a couple of times, but have always had reservations about using it on others. It's a highly effective way to remove pain, but pain is always present for a reason, and someone might avoid getting medical treatment after the pain has gone. Even if they do visit a doctor, the absence of pain will hinder the diagnosis. This technique removes pain, but it's not a cure.

Your pendulum can also help you identify the emotions and feelings that are often the underlying cause of illnesses. This is discussed in the next pages.

42. Resolving Long-Standing Emotions and Feelings

All of us, without exception, have minds full of outmoded beliefs and ideas, many of them dating back to early childhood. Some of these are conscious, but most are unconscious. Longstanding feelings of worthlessness or unworthiness, for instance, may have been created by the comments of others, negative experiences, or fears passed on to us from our parents and other people we're close to.

Have you ever found yourself in a situation having tried everything, but nothing worked? Have you almost succeeded at something, yet somehow sabotaged yourself and ended up worse off than you were before you started? The chances are it's not you, but your subconscious beliefs that are holding you back.

Have you ever said phrases to yourself like, "I'm stupid," "I'm always last," "I'll always be alone," "No one cares about me," "I don't deserve to be rich," and "I'm safe only when I make other people happy"? If so, your subconscious beliefs are preventing you from leading the life you should be living.

For about forty years, I thought I was hopeless at languages, because a teacher in high school told me I was. When I finally decided to learn another language, I was surprised that I was actually good at it. I'd allowed this false belief to hold me back for decades.

I know a highly talented artist who always denigrates her own work. "It's really not very good," she'll say when someone compliments her. "I'm hopeless at painting." This woman is in her mid-forties. She's won a number of awards and her paintings hang in galleries in several countries. By any standard, she's a successful artist, and everyone believes it except her.

At a funeral I went to recently, I learned that a man who'd spent almost all of his spare time trying to become a writer had died without publishing anything. I'd known him for more than thirty years and he'd never mentioned his dream of becoming a writer to me. His widow told me afterward that he'd never tried to get anything published, as he didn't think he'd written anything good enough to send to a publisher.

Negative feelings about money are common too. These usually come from our parents and date back to childhood. They might have told you, "We can't afford that," "Money doesn't grow on trees," "Good people aren't rich," "Life is a struggle," "Money is the root of all evil," "It's better to give than to receive," and so on. Even if you regularly say prosperity affirmations to yourself, these negative affirmations will lurk in your subconscious mind waiting to sabotage you at every opportunity.

There must be untold millions of people around the world who consciously or subconsciously believe they're not good enough, and consequently fail to achieve their dreams.

Many of these beliefs go back to early childhood experiences. Were you ever told, "People can't be trusted," "Big boys don't cry," "Children should be seen and not heard," "You're stupid," "Don't do as I do, do as I say," or "You're just jealous"? Sadly, these old beliefs remain in the subconscious and affect every aspect of the person's life.

You might even be creating new false beliefs by thinking thoughts like "I hate my body," "I'll never find a loving partner," "Men only want me for sex," "Life's unfair," "I never get a break," "I'm always unlucky," and "If people knew how I felt, no one would ever want to know me."

In addition to thoughts such as these, you might have numerous subconscious beliefs that are also holding you back. Fortunately, your pendulum will help you uncover any hidden negative thoughts or feelings. Once you know what they are, you'll be able to eliminate them from your life.

Start by making a list of what's important to you. It doesn't matter how long or short your list is. You might, for instance, write "love, home, travel, health, knowledge, money."

Hold your pendulum over the first item on your list (love, in our example). Ask, "Do I have any subconscious fears or beliefs about relationships?" If your pendulum gives a negative response, move on to the second item.

If it gives a positive response, use your pendulum to examine this further to find out what the fears or beliefs are. You might start by asking if these beliefs came as a result of one or more past relationships. You could ask if your negative beliefs about relationships came from observing your parents' relationship. You might ask if you believe you can ever have a successful relationship. Ask if you're prepared to put everything you have into the right relationship to ensure it is successful. Continue asking questions until you understand why you can't sustain a relationship. Once you know what it is, you can spin your pendulum counterclockwise and ask it to eliminate this unwanted, outmoded belief.

Instead of asking questions, you could write another list, this time thinking about the word *relationships* and writing down every thought that comes into your mind. Hold your pendulum over each of these in turn to see which, if any, is connected with an unwanted belief. When you find out what it is, swing your pendulum counterclockwise and ask it to neutralize and eliminate it.

Another possibility is to forego the questioning and ask your pendulum to eliminate the negative beliefs without discovering what they are. There's nothing wrong with this. Some people want to know exactly what is holding them back, while others want to let go of the negativity and not concern themselves with what caused it in the first place.

It's not enough to simply remove the false belief or emotion. You need to replace it with something positive and worthwhile. Let's assume that your pendulum reacted negatively when you held it over *money*, and you find out that you've been holding on to a belief that you don't deserve to be rich. Once you've eliminated that false belief, you might replace it with the complete opposite: the belief that you deserve to be rich.

Here's how you might do it. Swing your pendulum counterclockwise and say words along the lines of these:

> I ask the Universal Life Force to completely remove all the false thoughts and beliefs I've had about money, particularly my belief that I don't deserve to be rich. I know now that money is just money. It's neither good nor bad. It just is. I have just as much right to abundance as anyone else. Consequently, I've had enough of this disgusting limiting belief that's been holding me back and preventing me from showing the world what I can do. I let go of all my old thoughts and beliefs about money, and ask the Universal Life Force to help me to totally, completely, and irrevocably eliminate these limiting beliefs. Thank you. Thank you. Thank you.

Continue talking in this way until your pendulum stops moving. Say thank you one more time. Pause for a minute or two. You might like to drink a glass of water or eat a few nuts or raisins before continuing. When you're ready, swing your pendulum clockwise and instill the positive beliefs about money that you want to accept into your mind, body, and spirit. Say:

> I thank the Universal Life Force for eliminating all my old negative thoughts about money. I realize now that I deserve just as much of the good things of life as anyone else, and I ask you to help me achieve this goal by filling every cell of my body with positive thoughts and beliefs about money, wealth, and abundance. Please help me develop a prosperity consciousness that will attract money to me. Please encourage me to believe in myself and my abilities. I deserve to be rich in every sense of the word. Thank you for blessing my life with prosperity and success. Thank you. Thank you. Thank you.

Test yourself regularly to make sure that all your old negative beliefs about money have been neutralized and replaced with positive thoughts and beliefs about wealth, prosperity, and abundance.

43. The Pendulum and Affirmations

Every day we have a mixture of positive and negative thoughts. Thoughts are incredibly powerful and it's important to our well-being that we have more positive thoughts than negative ones.

Affirmations are positive statements that are always framed in the present tense and are said strongly as if you already possess the desired quality. They're always stated enthusiastically and firmly to help imprint the thought into your subconscious mind. Affirmations are repeated over and over again until they're accepted by your subconscious mind and become a reality.

You can create affirmations about almost anything. You can create an affirmation to help you lose weight, overcome fears and phobias, stop bad habits, find the right partner, obtain the right job, change personality traits, enjoy good health, travel wherever you want to go, increase your income, and much, much more. Here are some examples:

- I attract abundance in all areas of my life.

- I am enthusiastic and positive.

- I love others and others love me.

- My life is filled with love.

- I love my body and look after it with regular exercise and good quality food.

- I accomplish my goals.

- I am successful.

- I have all the money I need.

- I deserve to be rich.

- I am kind and treat myself and others with respect and love.

- I accept myself unconditionally.

- Day by day, in every way, I'm getting better and better.

You can find plenty of affirmations online. Test each one that interests you with your pendulum. If the pendulum gives a negative response to an affirmation, repeat the affirmation to yourself whenever you can for a day or two. Choose a time when you feel relaxed and rested. Hold your pendulum, close your eyes, and say the affirmation ten times, using as much enthusiasm as you can. Emphasize a different word each time you say it. When you open your eyes, you'll hopefully see your pendulum now giving the positive response. If not, repeat this exercise regularly until you get the response you desire.

It's easy to find a readymade affirmation, but it's usually better to create a good, strong affirmation that reflects exactly what you want. Keep it brief and write it in the present tense. Once you've done that, you need to repeat it as often as you can.

The theory is simple, but many people find it hard to make it work in practice. An example would be someone who is regularly affirming "money comes to me easily and effortlessly." They might be saying this a thousand times a day, but if their subconscious mind doesn't believe what they're affirming, nothing will happen until they eliminate their current negative feelings about money (see the section on resolving long-standing emotions and feelings on page 200).

Fortunately, there are ways to eliminate negative beliefs and feelings. Once you've done that, you can ask questions about any affirmations before deciding whether or not to adopt them.

Here's an exercise to help you choose the right affirmations for you.

1. Write several possible affirmations on individual pieces of paper. Hold your pendulum over one of these, and ask, "Is this a good affirmation for me to use at this time?" If your pendulum gives a positive response, move on to the next step. If you get a negative response, hold your pendulum over the other affirmations, one at a time, until one of them gives a positive response.

2. With your pendulum still held over the affirmation, ask, "Are there any blocks in my mind, body, or spirit that will prevent my subconscious mind from accepting this affirmation?" A negative response

shows that you're still hanging on to an outmoded belief about the content of the affirmation. This needs to be removed before you go on to the next step.

3. Ask: "Will my subconscious mind accept this affirmation and make it real?" You need to get a positive response to this question before you can start using the affirmation. If you get a negative response, you'll need to ask further questions to find out why your subconscious mind is rejecting the affirmation.

4. Say the affirmation out loud and see if your pendulum gives a positive response. It's a sign that your subconscious mind is willing to accept the affirmation if you get a positive response. Repeat the previous steps if you receive a negative response at this stage.

5. Swing your pendulum clockwise, and continue saying your affirmation until the pendulum stops. You can say the affirmation silently, but it's better to say it out loud if possible. This is because you'll hear yourself saying the words, adding an additional sense to the process. Use as much energy and forcefulness as you can while saying the affirmation. Emphasize a different word each time you say it. Say your affirmations softly, loudly, and with a variety of different tones of voice. A friend of mine

who is a good mimic says his affirmations using a different regional accent each time.

Once your pendulum stops moving, say, "Thank you, Universal Life Force. Thank you. Thank you. Thank you."

Repeat the affirmation as often as you can. You might say it silently whenever you have a spare moment, such as while you're waiting for a traffic signal to change or waiting in line. Say it in bed at night, say it in the shower. Say it any time you have a spare moment. At least once a day, repeat step five and say it while your pendulum is revolving in clockwise circles. Continue doing this until the affirmation is part of your belief system and you're receiving the benefits of it.

You might like to write your affirmation on a card that you can carry with you. You can look at it and silently repeat the words whenever you have a few spare moments. At least once a day, go somewhere private and hold your pendulum over your affirmation. Say the affirmation, preferably out loud, and follow it by saying "Yes! Yes! Yes!" Your pendulum will give a positive response to this. Watch the pendulum and when it starts to slow down, say your affirmation and the three yeses again. Repeat this several times to feed your subconscious mind with your desire. You'll find this an extremely effective way to increase the power of your affirmation.

44. Controlling Stress

An old joke says that the only people who don't suffer from stress are in graveyards. As we all experience challenges in our lives, no one can escape stress. However, it needs to be kept under control, as stress affects the physical body and can cause a wide variety of problems, ranging all the way from tension headaches to death.

Stress has always been necessary for survival. In an emergency, for instance, the adrenal glands increase our breathing, tense our muscles, and release fats and sugar to provide instant energy. This prepares our muscles for activity, and improves sight and hearing. This was essential in caveman times when survival depended on quick reflexes and instant action. In the world we live in today, an emergency might not involve any physical activity. In fact, in the workplace we may have to conceal the fact that we're stressed. Usually, once the stressful moment is over, our heart rate goes down, our bodies gradually return to normal, and life carries on.

However, if the stress is ongoing, as it can be in many workplaces, and in life-changing situations such as divorce or redundancy, we're likely to suffer from headaches, shortness of breath, stomach pain, high blood pressure, heart palpitations, ulcers, and a whole host of other physical problems. Prolonged stress can also cause anxiety and depression.

Chronic work stress, also known as career burnout, has a negative effect on our physical, mental, and emotional well-being. It's often created by lack of job security, endless demands, bullying, personality conflicts, and a lack of control over how our work is done.

As we cannot avoid stress, we need to develop a way of handling it so that it doesn't affect us physically. Regular exercise, healthy food, and sufficient sleep are essential. We also need to spend leisure time with family and friends, or doing something pleasurable such as reading a book or enjoying a leisurely bath.

Your pendulum can help you control your stress levels. It can also provide advice on what you need to do to handle any stress that occurs in your everyday life. In addition to using it to answer questions about whatever is causing the stress, it will also help you eliminate much of it. You do this by revolving your pendulum counterclockwise while asking it to eliminate all the negativity that's surrounding you. When it stops moving, revolve it again clockwise and ask the Universal Light Force to fill you with positivity and boundless energy. Do this at least once a day whenever you're facing serious stress. You can also perform this exercise on a regular basis to eliminate all the minor stresses that you experience in your everyday life.

The best tools to handle stress are diet, exercise, and relaxation. Unfortunately, these are all things that tend to be forgotten when people experience prolonged stress. Many people automatically seek comfort in fatty foods, sugar, caffeine, rich foods, and alcohol when they're suffering from stress. Unfortunately, these foods are likely to increase, rather than reduce, your stress levels. The best foods to eat while suffering from stress are bland, low-fat, easily digested foods. Follow the suggestions in the pendulum and your diet chapter on page 188, and add any questions you wish, regarding what foods are good to eat while you're suffering from stress.

Even though everyone knows they need to exercise to remain fit and healthy, few people make the time or effort to do it. Apart from its health benefits, exercise helps reduce stress levels. Make a list of all the possible forms of exercise you could do, and ask your pendulum about each one. Choose a form of exercise that you enjoy, and, if you can, exercise with a friend.

Relaxation is also important. Stress dramatically increases tension, and this makes it hard to relax properly. This is why people suffering from stress often find it hard to sleep. Deep breathing is a good way to reduce tension and stress. Take several slow, deep breaths, hold them for several seconds, and slowly exhale.

You might prefer to lie on your back, close your eyes, and gradually relax all the muscles in your body, starting with either your head or your feet.

You can also relax by spending time with friends, pursuing a hobby, singing, or doing anything else you enjoy.

Again, make a list and ask your pendulum which forms of relaxation would be most beneficial for you.

45. Map Dowsing with Your Pendulum

In the introduction, I mentioned Verne Cameron and how he'd used a pendulum to locate the positions and depths of all the submarines in the Pacific Ocean at that time. In the 1940s, Henry Gross located the site of the first freshwater well in Bermuda. He did this from his home in Maine. (Roberts 1951.) Abbé Mermet located oil, minerals, and water in Africa and South America by map dowsing. He also did archaeological dowsing for the Vatican, and found missing people with the help of his pendulum.

Sadly, many of these people were dead before he was asked to find them, but at least some had a happy ending. In January 1935, a woman in France asked him to try to find her twenty-six-year-old son who had disappeared. Using maps and his pendulum, Abbé Mermet was able to tell the distraught mother that her son had had a nervous breakdown and was in Toulouse, forty-five miles away. Ten days later, the Abbé received a letter from the mother, saying that "they were making arrangements for his return home" (Mermet 1959, 202-203).

In 1970, not long before he became the world's most famous psychic, Uri Geller used his map dowsing skills to help Moshe Dayan, at that time the Israeli Minister of Defense, locate archaeological treasures, which the minister later displayed in his home. He wasn't paid for doing so, but since then Uri Geller has become the highest paid map dowser in history. In 1986, *The Financial Times* in London reported that Uri Geller received one million pounds for every job of map dowsing he undertook (Jacobsen 2017, 332).

There are a number of ways to perform map dowsing, and many dowsers use a combination of all them.

The first method is to move the pendulum over a map until the pendulum reacts. Continue doing this with more localized maps to pinpoint the exact location. Some dowsers prefer to use a pen or pencil as a pointer, and pass this over the map while the other hand holds the pendulum to one side. The pendulum reacts when the pointer is over the right spot.

The second method is similar to the first. Hold your pendulum beside the map and move a ruler or some other straight edge across the map until the pendulum reacts. Draw a fine pencil line across the map to mark where the pendulum reacted. Repeat the process by moving the ruler down the map at a ninety-degree angle to the drawn line. Draw another line when the pendulum reacts. You'll find the item where the two lines intersect.

The third method involves placing the pendulum over one of the bottom corners of the map and asking it to indicate the direction of whatever it is you are searching for. The pendulum will swing to indicate a particular direction. Draw a pencil line across the map using the edge of your ruler. Repeat the process from the other bottom corner. You will find what you are searching for where the two lines intersect.

A fourth and similar method uses the map coordinates. Ask your pendulum, "Where on the north-south coordinate is (whatever it is you are divining for) to be found?" As you are saying this, run your pointer down the map from north to south. Mark where the pendulum responds. Repeat the process going from west to east. The item you are searching for will be found where the coordinates meet.

The fifth method involves mentally dividing the map into quarters. Hold the pendulum over each quarter in turn, and ask: "Will I find (whatever it is you're searching for) in this square?" The pendulum will react when it's over the right one. This quarter is again divided into quarters, and the process repeated. This can be done again and again, preferably using more localized maps, until the exact spot is located. Many maps are divided into grids, and you may prefer to use these instead of the quarters.

You don't necessarily need an accurate map to perform map dowsing. Bob Ater, a well-known dowser in Maine, was challenged by two reporters, Emily and Per Ola d'Aulaire, at a dowsing convention in 1975. They handed him a sketched map, drawn in pencil on the back of an envelope, and told him it was a map of their farm, three hundred miles away in Connecticut. They asked him to tell them where their water well was. He successfully showed them where it was. He then told them there was an oblong shape on their property and indicated a blank area of their map. The reporters couldn't think what it could be, until one remembered it was the foundations of an old garage that used to be on the site. Finally, Bob Ater ran his pencil along the outline of the house and found a "snaky line." The reporters were startled, as they realized he'd located their garden hose, exactly where they'd left it (article in *Saturday Evening Post*, May/June 1976).

A couple of years ago, my wife and I spent a few days at a seaside resort town and met a couple who owned a craft store there. When I said how fortunate they were to live in such a beautiful place, the husband told us they'd found it by using luck and magic. He was busy serving customers, so we had to visit their store again later to learn more. He and his wife had been high school teachers. They loved their work, but had grown tired of the long daily commutes and the hustle and bustle of life in a big city. One evening, he opened up a map of the entire country and asked his pendulum to find them the perfect place to live. When he ran his pendulum along the vertical and horizontal coordinates it indicated the resort town.

They did nothing about it for almost a year. It became almost a joke. Whenever one of them got caught up in gridlock traffic, he or she would suggest they move to this town that they had yet to visit. Finally, they went there on vacation and fell in love with it right away. After asking their pendulum further questions about the wisdom of making such a big move, they resigned from their positions, sold their house, and moved.

"It was the best thing we've ever done," he told me. "We were planning to find teaching positions here, but this store came on the market at the right time. We bought a house just up the road, so we walk to work. No more commuting! We love the climate here, too. We're very happy."

46. Dowsing Photographs

Not long ago, my wife was looking for a particular photo in an old photograph album, and found a photo that had been accidentally misfiled. The people in the photo were quite a bit older than they were in the photographs that surrounded it. I managed to date it with the help of my pendulum, and we were able to place it where it should have been, in a different album.

I thought nothing of this until we happened to mention it to a friend who was fascinated with what we'd done. She asked many questions, and a few days later visited us with a box of photos she was curious about. I showed her how I did it, and gave her a pendulum to practice with. She turned out to be a natural dowser and is now using the pendulum in many areas of her life.

You can do much more than date photographs with your pendulum. You can ask questions about the setting of the photograph. You can learn about the people in the picture. Some dowsers pick up on these people's hopes, dreams, disappointments, and triumphs, as well as the state of their health and degree of satisfaction with life.

However, there can be ethical problems in doing this. I'm happy to dowse photographs of people who are deceased without permission, but would need agreement from the person in the photograph to dowse someone who is still alive.

If the photograph includes enough land, you can use it as a map when you're dowsing for water or anything else.

Abbé Mermet was able to diagnose illnesses by dowsing photographs with his pendulum. He believed that the photograph indicated the state of the person at the moment the photograph was taken, and also indicated the present state of the person. It could, for instance, tell if the person was healthy, unwell, or dead.

In April 1935, the *Courier de Genève* reported an example of Abbé Mermet's skills with the pendulum. The family of an engineer who had disappeared while traveling on business contacted the Abbé to see if he could find out what had happened to him. Abbé Mermet suspended his pendulum over a photograph of the missing man and a map of the area. After doing this, he was able to tell the man's relatives that after enjoying dinner in a restaurant in the town of Valence, he'd gone for a walk and had accidentally fallen into the Rhône River. The river had carried the body downstream to Aramon where it had become lodged in a crevice. The relatives went to the place the Abbé indicated and found his body (Mermet 1959, 199-200).

47. Weather Forecasting with the Pendulum

The weather is a perennially interesting topic of conversation, and sooner or later people tend to discuss the inaccuracy of weather forecasts. Meteorologists are used to this, as a tiny change in one area of the country can make a huge difference somewhere else, destroying what was, until then, an accurate weather forecast.

I know several people who ignore the published weather forecasts and do their own, using a pendulum. All of them started doing this because they were dissatisfied with the accuracy of the published forecasts. They usually concern themselves with the weather in their local area, but I know one person who dowses about a dozen cities around the world. He does this as a hobby, and he enjoys comparing his forecasts with what actually occurs.

Although the dowsers I know usually work only a day or two ahead, dowsing the weather is extremely useful if you're planning an outdoor activity weeks or months ahead. As well as finding out the chances of rain or snow, you might like to ask your pendulum how many hours of sunshine you'll have, and what the temperature will be at certain times of the day.

48. Dowsing for Water, Oil, and Minerals

When people think of dowsing, they usually think of water divining, and most professional dowsers make the majority of their income from doing this. There are many examples of people who have found water in locations that were thought to be arid.

General George S. Patton is said to have used a dowser to find fresh drinking water for his troops in North Africa after the Germans blew up all the wells (Schmicker 2002, 121).

In the 1980s, the German government sponsored a ten-year research program into dowsing. During this, they performed over two thousand drillings in Kenya, Namibia, Sri Lanka, Yemen, and Zaire. 691 of these test drillings were done in Sri Lanka, and the dowsers were successful 96 percent of the time. In most cases, the dowsers also predicted the depth of the well and the volume of water within ten to twenty percent. Most of these drill sites were in areas where the chances of finding water randomly were extremely low (Miller).

Dowsers are called "doodlebuggers" in the petroleum industry. Paul Clement Brown, an MIT graduate and electrical engineer, was one of the most famous of these. His favorite tool was the pendulum. He located oil for many companies, including Getty Oil, Mobil Oil, Signal Oil, and

Standard Oil. Chet Davis, a petroleum engineer, was skeptical and tested him on thirty-five sites. "He was right on all thirty-five sites," he reported afterward. "I don't think anyone in the oil business would believe it if they didn't see it. I wouldn't have" (http://jimmyjoeault.wixsite.com/adventures/single-post/2014/06/19/Dowsing-For-Oil).

In 2017, The Independent, a leading UK newspaper, reported that engineers in ten of twelve water companies occasionally used dowsing rods to find pipes or detect leaks (Sharman 2017).

You can dowse for water with your pendulum. Remember to be specific as far as the quantity and quality of water you want. If you're searching over a large area, such as a farm, you might want to map dowse in preference to walking all over the property. You can start by pinpointing the exact position on a map, and then visit the site to confirm what your pendulum has told you.

Once you've found a vein of usable water, your pendulum will also tell you how far below the surface it is and the volume of water that's available.

The easiest method to determine depth is to stand over the vein with your pendulum in your hand. Say: "I need to know how far down the water is. Is it ten feet? Is it twenty feet?" Continue asking questions about the depth until your pendulum reacts. Let's assume it reacts when you reach one hundred and thirty feet. This tells you that the water is between 125 and 135 feet below the surface.

The final step is to determine the yield. This is important, because if it's too small it may not be worthwhile to drill the well. Stand over the vein and ask, "How many gallons of water per minute will this vein provide? Ten gallons? Twenty gallons?" Your pendulum will react when you reach the nearest ten gallons.

49. Remote Dowsing

Remote dowsing occurs when the dowser is in one location and whatever he or she is dowsing for is situated somewhere else. Map dowsing is a form of remote dowsing, as you can sit comfortably at home and use your pendulum to dowse a map of any part of the world.

However, with remote dowsing you don't need a map, a photograph, a plan, or anything other than your pendulum and your questions. Consequently, you can use it to dowse the North Pole, a house on the other side of the world, the rings of Saturn, or anywhere else that interests you. You can dowse people, animals, and plants too. You can even locate geopathic stress. There are no limits to where or what you can dowse remotely.

Obviously, there is an ethical issue here, as there is in all forms of dowsing. You should never use dowsing to secretly find out what someone is doing without their permission, even if they are on the other side of the world. Similarly, you can't use it to locate missing people, or even missing ships and aircraft, unless you have permission to do so. Abbé Mermet did a great deal of this sort of dowsing, but he always asked for permission first.

My late friend Brian Reid successfully dowsed for forgotten gravesites (Webster 1996, 164-165). As these were all at least a hundred years old, he did not need to ask anyone's permission. He did this voluntarily as a service to the community. On a number of occasions, he was asked by descendants to find an ancestor's grave.

I've met many people who can accept dowsing on site, but find it hard to imagine that people can dowse anywhere in the world with nothing but a pendulum. Presumably, dowsing in this way enables you to access the Universal Mind that knows everything. This makes it similar to remote viewing. However, like dowsing itself, no one has yet come up with an explanation for remote dowsing that is acceptable to everyone.

50. Dowsing from a List

It's always enjoyable to go out for dinner; my wife and I have a number of favorite restaurants that we visit every now and again. Sometimes, when I look at the menu I can tell right away what meal I'll choose. On other occasions, though, I find it hard to decide what to order. When this occurs, I select my meal using my pendulum. I don't make a show of this, and usually keep my pendulum out of sight below the table so that no one can see what I'm doing. If this isn't possible, I'll body dowse, using my fingers instead of my pendulum (see appendix).

To choose a meal, I read the menu and ask my pendulum, "Is there an item on this menu that will satisfy me in every way, and is an eight, nine, or ten on a scale from one to ten?" If the restaurant is of a good standard, I'm virtually certain to get a positive response. I then use my free hand to run a finger down the side of the menu, and the pendulum provides a yes response each time my finger indicates a meal it knows I'll enjoy.

If my pendulum indicates more than one item, I ask further questions to find the item my pendulum thinks will be best for me. If, for instance, my pendulum indicates items three, twelve, and seventeen on the menu, I'll ask, "Would I enjoy (item number three) more than (item number 12)?" Once I know which of these I'd prefer, I then ask the same question again using the name of that item and the name of number seventeen.

This is useful at restaurants, and I sometimes choose wine from the wine list in the same way. I also use it for many other purposes as well.

I might make a list of vacation destinations and dowse them in the same way I do with a menu. Recently, my wife was ordering some shoes online and couldn't decide which ones to order. We made a list of the shoes she liked and asked the pendulum which pair she would be happiest with. As the shoes were available in a variety of colors, we asked it to recommend the color she'd be happiest with as well.

I'm not a natural handyman, but enjoy browsing in home repair stores. These megastores have huge selections of virtually everything, and inevitably I have problems deciding what to buy. Nowadays, I go online first, make a list of what I want, and let my pendulum decide which one I'd be happiest with.

Way back, in pre-internet days, I'd ask my pendulum questions about tradespeople and suppliers who were listed in the Yellow Pages. Nowadays, I do this while doing an internet search instead.

Some years ago, I was telling a fellow dowser what I did, and he told me that he'd bought his car using the same process. He went online and did a search for the particular car he wanted. He found dozens of advertisements, and as he didn't have the time or inclination to check them all out, he used his pendulum to choose three. Before going to see any of them, he asked his pendulum to indicate the one that would be best for him. He looked at all three cars and bought the one his pendulum had indicated. When I asked him why he bothered looking at the other two, he told me that he did it for educational purposes. He learned a great deal about the model and specifications of the car he wanted from speaking to the owners and taking the cars for test drives. This enabled him to know what to look for and what questions he should ask when he spoke to the owner of the third car. This knowledge also enabled him to buy the car for considerably less than he thought he would.

CONCLUSION

By now, I hope you've discovered for yourself what an amazing instrument the pendulum is. However, like anything worthwhile, it takes practice to become good at using it. If you put time and effort into it, you'll become a good dowser and will be able to use these skills to help yourself and others.

When I was a child, my mother used to tie her wedding ring to a length of cotton thread and use that as a pendulum. Every time anyone we knew became pregnant, my mother would be asked if the baby would be a boy or a girl. The mother to be and her close relatives all came to watch as the pendulum indicated the gender of the unborn baby. I've no idea what my mother's success rate was, but can't remember her ever being wrong. My siblings and I thought nothing of it. Dowsing with a ring was a perfectly normal activity in our world. Consequently, I've never known a time when a pendulum wasn't part of my everyday life.

One of the reasons I wrote this book was because many dowsers use their pendulums for only one or two purposes. As far as I know, my mother never used her pendulum for anything other than determining the gender of unborn babies.

We've just looked at fifty ways to use a pendulum, but there are many, many more. Recently, I met someone who uses her pendulum to check her emails before she sends them. She asks if everything she's written is correct and if the recipient will be able to understand what she's written. If in doubt, she'll write a message twice and ask the pendulum to decide which one of them she should send. She also asks if and when the recipient will respond.

Another person told me he had an addictive personality. Over a period of time, he used his pendulum to free himself from his addictions, working on one of them at a time. He now conducts classes teaching other people how they can do the same.

I met an unusual man at a dowsing convention some years ago. He used his pendulum to decide if he needed to visit a dentist. He'd touch each of his teeth in turn while holding his pendulum in his other hand. He'd avoid visiting his dentist as long as his pendulum gave a positive response to each tooth. He'd make an appointment if his pendulum gave a negative response on any tooth.

Although the pendulum is an amazing instrument, you must use your common sense along with it. For all important decisions, you need to gather as much information as possible before making up your mind. You can use your pendulum as just one of the methods you use to gain insight into a situation.

Your pendulum will enhance your life in many ways, and you'll experience great joy and pleasure from using it to help yourself and others. I wish you great success with it.

APPENDIX:
BODY DOWSING

Body dowsing is known by several names, including propless dowsing, hand dowsing, toolless dowsing, and deviceless dowsing. No matter what name it's known by, it's a useful way to dowse when you don't have a pendulum or any other dowsing instrument available.

At times, you may not have your pendulum with you, or you may not want to attract attention to yourself by using your pendulum in public. Not everyone approves of dowsing, and over the years I've been called a variety of unpleasant names by people who think the pendulum is operated by the Devil. In situations of this sort, you can use your body, or part of it, instead of a pendulum.

If I'm standing, I'll use my whole body as a pendulum. I might, for instance, be in a bookstore and find it hard to decide which of two books to buy. I'll place one book slightly to my left and the other slightly to my right. I'll close my eyes and ask my body, "Which of these books will be more useful to me at this time?" I'll pause for a few seconds before opening my eyes. Although I'm not consciously aware that I moved at all, when I open my eyes I'll be looking at or leaning slightly toward the book I should buy.

You can use your body to provide yes and no answers too. Stand with your feet shoulder width apart and ask a couple of questions that you know the answers to, to see how your body provides positive and negative responses. Once you know these, you can ask your body any questions that can be answered with yes or no. When you first experiment with this, you'll probably find it easier to close your eyes. However, once you've gained experience, you'll be able to do this just as well with your eyes open.

The best way to practice body dowsing is to dowse for objects that you've already located with your pendulum. If, for instance, you used your pendulum to locate your water mains, go over the same ground again with your arms extended in front of you at shoulder height, and with your palms facing each other.

Take a few slow, deep breaths, think of the water mains, and slowly walk toward your water pipe. You may feel some tingling, itching, or some other involuntary movement in your hands as you get close to it. One arm might rise or bob up and down. A finger might twitch or vibrate rapidly. You could find that your hands start moving together until they almost touch. All of these are dowsing responses.

There are a number of different ways to dowse using your fingers. Place the tips of your thumb and forefinger of your nondominant hand together and mentally ask a question. After doing this, gently rub the fingers together. It's a positive response if the two fingers feel slightly sticky and won't slide easily over each other. It's a negative response if the two fingers slide easily together.

An alternative to this also uses your nondominant hand. Place your forefinger over your second finger. Ask your question and then slide the forefinger off the other finger. The answer is yes if the finger tends to stick and doesn't move easily. It's a no if the forefinger slides away easily.

Instead of sliding your thumb over your forefinger, you may prefer to slide it over a smooth surface, such as the side of a glass or a tumbled stone. You need to slide it extremely gently, with your thumb barely contacting the surface. It's a yes if your thumb sticks slightly when you do this and a no when it doesn't.

This method uses fingers from both hands. Make two joined circles by interlocking your thumbs and forefingers. Ask your question, then try to separate the circles by pulling your left hand away. It's a positive response if there's noticeable resistance when you try to separate your two hands after asking the question. If the hands separate easily, the answer is no.

In the late nineteenth century, a fourteen-year-old boy called Fred Rodwell achieved fame with his hand dowsing ability. He clasped his hands while dowsing. When he stood over the item he was dowsing for, his hands would lock together with such force that he couldn't separate them until he moved away (Barrett and Besterman 1968, 223-224).

Leicester Gataker, a well-known early twentieth-century dowser, would walk briskly over the area he was dowsing, with his arms down and slightly outward. When he got close to whatever he was dowsing for he'd experience a vibration in the middle fingers of each hand (Willey 1975, 52-54).

Many years ago, I met a professional dowser who claimed he could locate oil from an airplane flying at 30,000 feet. He would sit in his comfortable business class seat with his elbows by his sides and his hands facing each other in front of him. When the plane flew over a site where oil was, his hands would tremble violently and wouldn't stop until the plane had flown away from the site where he'd located oil. The coordinates of the locations where his hands trembled were recorded, and engineers and drillers from the company that employed him would check out the sites later.

I've met a number of people who use their eyes as dowsing instruments. They keep their eyes wide open while thinking of their question. The answer is yes if their eyes blink involuntarily.

The wrist twist is another method that works well for some people. Hold either hand out as if you were going to shake hands with someone. Ask the question. The hand will twist involuntarily in a clockwise direction if the answer is yes and counterclockwise if the answer is no.

With some people the dowsing response is reversed. When a dowser rubs his or her thumb against the forefinger it usually indicates yes if the thumb tends to stick and no if it slides easily. However, some dowsers find that the thumb sticking means no and the thumb sliding easily means yes. This reversed response can apply with all of the methods described here. Experiment and find out what your personal responses are.

BIBLIOGRAPHY

Alleyne, Richard. "Women's Voices 'Make Plants Grow Faster' Finds Royal Horticultural Society." *The Telegraph.* June 22, 2009. https://www.telegraph.co.uk /news/earth/earthnews/5602419/Womens-voices -make-plants-grow-faster-finds-Royal-Horticultural -Society.html.

Barbor, Cary. "The Science of Meditation." *Psychology Today* 34, no. 54 (2001).

Barrett, Sir William, and Theodore Besterman. *The Divining Rod.* New Hyde Park, NY: University Books, Inc., 1968.

Bird, Christopher. *The Divining Hand.* New York: E. P. Dutton, 1979.

Buckland, Raymond. *The Spirit Book: The Encyclopedia of Clairvoyance, Channeling, and Spirit Communication.* Canton, MI: Visible Ink Press, 2005.

Bulgatz, Joseph. *Ponzi Schemes, Invaders from Mars, and More Extraordinary Popular Delusions.* New York: Harmony Books, 1992.

Cameron, Verne L., Bill Cox, and Georgiana Teeple. *Map Dowsing: The Dowser's Handbook Series No. 1.* Santa Barbara, CA: El Cariso Publications, 1971.

Copen, Bruce. *The Practical Pendulum.* Sussex, UK: Academic Publications, 1974.

Cosimano, Charles W. *Psychic Power.* St. Paul, MN: Llewellyn Publications, 1992. Originally published as *Psionics 101.*

Cowan, David, and Eriana Cowan. *Dowsing beyond Reality: Access Your Power to Create Positive Change.* San Francisco: Weiser Books, 2012.

Eason, Cassandra. *The Art of the Pendulum.* York Beach, ME: Red Wheel/Weiser, 2005.

Elliot, J. Scott. *Dowsing One Man's Way.* Jersey, UK: Neville Spearman (Jersey) Limited, 1977.

Fairley, John, and Simon Welfare. *Arthur C. Clarke's World of Strange Powers.* London: HarperCollins, 1982.

Fodor, Nandor. *Encyclopedia of Psychic Science*. London: Arthurs Press, 1933. Reprinted New Hyde Park, NJ: University Books, Inc., 1974.

Friedman, Sidney. *Your Mind Knows More Than You Do: The Subconscious Secrets of Success*. Nevada City, CA: Blue Dolphin Publishing, Inc., 2000.

Friedmann, Erika, Aaron H. Katcher, Sue A. Thomas, James J. Lynch, and Peter R. Messent. "Animal Companions and One-Year Survival of Patients After Discharge from a Coronary Care Unit." *Public Health Report* 95 (1980).

Grace, Raymon. *The Future Is Yours*. Charlottesville, VA: Hampton Roads Publishing Company, 2003.

Hitching, Francis. *Pendulum: The Psi Connection*. London: Fontana Books, 1977.

Iacoboni, M. "Imitation, Empathy, and Mirror Neurons." *Annual Review of Psychology* 60 (2009): 653-670.

Jacobsen, Annie. *Phenomena: The Secret History of the U.S. Government's Investigations into Extrasensory Perception and Psychokinesis*. New York: Little, Brown and Company, 2017.

Lakhovsky, Georges. *The Secret of Life*. London: William Heinemann Limited, 1939.

Lethbridge, T. C. *The Power of the Pendulum*. London: Routledge & Kegan Paul plc, 1976.

Long, Max Freedom. *Psychometric Analysis*. Vista, CA: Huna Research Publications, 1959.

Mayer, Elizabeth Lloyd. *Extraordinary Knowing: Science, Skepticism and the Inexplicable Powers of the Human Mind*. New York: Bantam Books, 2008.

Mermet, Abbé Alexis. *Principles and Practice of Radiesthesia*. London: Vincent Stuart Publishers Ltd., 1959.

Miller, Anne. "Dowsing: A Review." The Scientific & Medical Network. https://explore.scimednet.org/index.php/dowsing-a-review/

Nielsen, Greg, and Joseph Polansky. *Pendulum Power*. New York: Inner Traditions International Ltd., 1977.

Paine, Sheila. *Amulets: A World of Secret Powers, Charms and Magic*. London: Thames & Hudson Limited, 2004.

Roberts, Kenneth. *Henry Gross and His Dowsing Rod*. Garden City, NY: Doubleday and Company, 1951.

Schmicker, Michael. *Best Evidence*. Bloomington, IN: iUniverse, 2002.

Sharman, Jon. "UK Water Companies Still Use 'Magic' Dowsing Rods to Find Leaks, Despite No Supporting Scientific Evidence." *Independent*. November 22, 2017. https://www.independent.co.uk/news/uk/home-news/

uk-water-companies-magic-dowsing-rods-use
-engineers-leaks-no-scientific-evidence-sally-le
-page-a8069616.html.

Staffen, Joan Rose. *The Book of Pendulum Healing: Charting Your Healing Course for Mind, Body & Spirit*. Red Wheel/Weiser, 2019.

Trinder, W. H. *Dowsing*. London: British Society of Dowsers, 1955.

Webster, Richard. *Dowsing for Beginners*. St. Paul: Llewellyn Publications, 1996.

Webster, Richard. *Pendulum Magic for Beginners*. Woodbury, MN: Llewellyn Publications, 2002.

———. *Psychic Protection for Beginners*. Woodbury, MN: Llewellyn Publications, 2010.

Willey, Raymond C. *Modern Dowsing*. Cottonwood, AZ: Esoteric Publications, 1975.

Williamson, Tom. *Dowsing: New Light on an Ancient Art*. London: Robert Hale Limited, 1993.

Wilson, Colin. *Beyond the Occult: Twenty Years' Research into the Paranormal*. London, UK: Bantom Press, 1988.

Woods, Walt. *Letter to Robin: A Mini-Course in Pendulum Dowsing*. http://lettertorobin.org.

To Write to the Author

If you wish to contact the author or would like more information about this book, please write to the author in care of Llewellyn Worldwide Ltd. and we will forward your request. Both the author and the publisher appreciate hearing from you and learning of your enjoyment of this book and how it has helped you. Llewellyn Worldwide Ltd. cannot guarantee that every letter written to the author can be answered, but all will be forwarded. Please write to:

Richard Webster
℅ Llewellyn Worldwide
2143 Wooddale Drive
Woodbury, MN 55125-2989
Please enclose a self-addressed stamped envelope for reply,
or $1.00 to cover costs. If outside the U.S.A., enclose
an international postal reply coupon.

Many of Llewellyn's authors have websites with additional information and resources. For more information, please visit our website at http://www.llewellyn.com.